Christian Life and Today's World

not conformed but transformed

Scripture Union

Christian Life and Today's World

not conformed but transformed

Scripture Union, 207–209 Queensway, Bletchley, MK2 2EB, England.
Email: info@scriptureunion.org.uk
Website: www.scriptureunion.org.uk
© Copyright Scripture Union 2002
First published 2002

ISBN 1 85999 560 8

The right of Antony Billington, Ailish Eves, Conrad Gempf, Peter Hicks, Tony Lane, Graham MacFarlane, Jane Rennie, Peter Riddell, Anna Robbins, Derek Tidball and Max Turner to be identified as authors of this work has been asserted by them in accordance with the Copyright, Designs and Patents Act 1988.

British Library Cataloguing-in-Publication Data
A catalogue record for this book is available from the British Library.

Cover design by David Lund
Printed and bound in Great Britain by Cox and Wyman Ltd.

Scripture Union
We are an international Christian charity working with churches in more than 130 countries providing resources to bring the good news about Jesus Christ to children, young people and families – and to encourage them to develop spiritually through the Bible and prayer.

As well as our network of volunteers, staff and associates who run holidays, church-based events and school Christian groups, we produce a wide range of publications and support those who use our resources through training programmes.

Contents

The authours

Chapter 1
Ailish Eves is Lecturer in Missiology and New Testament
Conrad Gempf is Lecturer in New Testament

Chapter 2
Tony Lane is Director of Research and Professor of
Historical Theology

Chapter 3
Max Turner is Vice Principal and Professor of
New Testament Studies

Chapter 4
Antony Billington is Lecturer in Hermeneutics

Chapter 5
Derek Tidball is Principal and Senior Lecturer in Sociology
of Religion

Chapter 6
Anna Robbins is Lecturer in Theology and Contemporary
Culture

Chapter 7
Graham McFarlane is Lecturer in Systematic Theology

Chapter 8
Conrad Gempf is Lecturer in New Testament

Chapter 9
Peter Hicks is Director of Ministry and Lecturer in
Theology

Chapter 10
Peter Riddell is Director of the Centre for Islamic Studies
and Muslim-Christian Relations, and Senior Lecturer in
Islam and Linguistics. He was interviewed by Anna Robbins.

Preface

Life in today's world seems to progress with such speed that we barely have time to digest one set of changes before another is upon us. Just keeping up with the pace of technological advancement and cultural shift requires immense effort and moral resourcefulness. Often we wonder what's happened to the world around us: it barely resembles the one we knew as children, let alone the world which Jesus entered and which we have had described to us in Scripture. We struggle to make sense of the challenges which come to our faith through contemporary culture, and we are uncertain about how to communicate Christ in ways that are relevant and effective. Yet, the influences of culture are so much a part of us that we fail sometimes to recognise their existence, and how inextricably linked to culture we really are. As Christians, we are children of God's Kingdom, and yet we are children of today's world. We embody so many tensions between them that it becomes difficult to sort out the temporal from the eternal, the meaningful from the insignificant. How do we understand the challenges of contemporary culture in order to respond biblically and faithfully? How do we interact with contemporary challenges in such a way that God is honoured and bridges are built to our neighbours and communities?

When we consider some of the challenges of living as Christians in today's world, we may become fearful or overwhelmed. The influences of culture seem to pursue us relentlessly, and we often become numb to their constant bombardment on our lives. Sometimes we avoid confrontation, hoping that if we keep busy enough, or ignore the challenges long enough, maybe they'll go away. But in reality, we cannot avoid culture's claims upon us. They are part of our day-to-day living, encountered in shopping malls, on television, in supermarkets, cinemas, schools, churches and workplaces, and in the thoughts and feelings which form in our own hearts and minds. They are a part of us just as we are part of them – which is why it becomes so difficult to reach an understanding of how to be in the world, and not of it.

This book emerged out of a desire to identify several major influences which both feed and grow out of contemporary culture, and understand them from a Christian perspective. The various ways in which these topics themselves are addressed by contemporary evangelical scholars reveals just how impossible it may be to separate completely the various strands which comprise faith and culture. And yet this fact itself emphasises the importance of the present task for understanding how culture influences the church and the ways the church seeks to respond to such challenges. Along with a video and study guide for small groups, this book comprises part of the second in a series of LBC-produced resources dealing with issues of contemporary Christian life. Several members of the London Bible College faculty have contributed articles to this book in an attempt to help Christians reflect biblically, and on some major themes of contemporary culture in today's world. From disciplines as diverse as biblical studies, theology, sociology, missiology, and ethics, we have attempted to facilitate the engagement of culture for all Christians who are concerned to offer a thoughtful, biblical response to today's faith challenges. As a diverse group of people, we represent differing perspectives on culture and the desired response to its challenges. Yet, our common commitment to Christ and desire to make him known in every culture unites us in heart and purpose. It is hoped that these efforts will bear fruit in the lives of many who will not only read this book, but use it as a catalyst for further ventures into faith and culture.

This segment of the *Christian Life and Today's World* project was conceived and made possible as the result of collaboration across many areas of the London Bible College and beyond. Special thanks goes to Jane Rennie for her vision in initiating the project; to Rob Purbrick and Tim Dendy of LBC Video for creativity and many hours spent in brain-storming sessions; to the principal, Derek Tidball, for allowing the freedom to develop the project, and his encouragement in seeing it through; and to members of the faculty for their careful work, and willingness to participate. The patience of Andrew Clark at Scripture Union was as graceful as it was long-suffering, and the careful attention of Jo Campbell to the manuscript was much appreciated. All concerned have made the process as enjoyable as it was educative, and it has been a privilege to see this volume through to press.

Today's world may look very different from the world into which Christ was born – indeed, into which we were born. But there is no doubt that it is the same world for which he died, and in which his Spirit is working today. For that reason alone, we must take up the present challenge and strive to understand our culture and the relationship of the church to it in order that we might faithfully engage the great commission to go into all the world – today's world – to be and make disciples, to the honour and glory of God.   *Anna Robbins*

Chapter 1

Presenting the challenge: Confronting culture

Ailish Eves and Conrad Gempf

Christians should be conscious of living with dual citizenship. Although we are not of the world, we are called to live in it; and this will, for most Christians, entail knowing and participating in their culture rather than remaining sealed off from it. The challenge is to remain focused on eternal realities while living in the present. Paul's example is of someone who knows culture well and uses that knowledge and participation not to "blend in with" but to critique culture.

Living the dual life

Like fish who never actually think about the water they are swimming in, we human beings tend not to realise that we are immersed in a culture until or unless we run up against one that is different. And you have only to spend a short time in another culture, or with someone from another culture, before the surprises start popping like camera flashes all around you, both blinding and illuminating at the same time. 'But *we* don't do things that way!' 'I never thought about it before.'

It is not unusual to feel this way at conversion: 'If anyone is in Christ, he is a new creation; the old has gone, the new has come!' (2 Cor 5:17). Do you remember feeling that everything had changed as a result of your new relationship with the Lord? Things that you held close to you in your 'previous life' suddenly seemed things that you not only could, but probably should, do without. I gave away most of my collection of hard rock LPs.

I had exchanged one kind of lifestyle for another – a kind of churchy, Jesus-freaky way of living.

Perhaps cultural vertigo still happens to you from time to time, perhaps it doesn't. If it doesn't, perhaps you nostalgically long for it to recur. At one time things were so fresh and new – you felt so different from your mates, their lifestyles and, most of all, their values – but it's fair to wonder what has really changed. I gave away my Steppenwolf LPs, and bought Larry Norman ones instead. From those bass lines that escaped my bedroom, my mother couldn't really tell the difference. I had exchanged one kind of lifestyle for another – a kind of churchy, Jesus-freaky way of living. I still liked the music, and still closed my bedroom door to play it loud. I was not so divorced from my culture and subculture as I felt myself to be. It is just not possible to be 'culture-less'.

There is a great deal that does change when someone becomes a Christian, but the New Testament appears not to endorse 'defection from the world' – or even, for most people, rejection of it – so much as the idea of continuing to be in the world but not of it (John 17:6–26). 'Our citizenship is in heaven' (Phil 3:20) it is true, but we remain, no less, people who live and act on the earth – people with a dual citizenship, acting and affecting both realms at once. Whatever we bind or loose on earth stands bound or loosed in heaven as well (Matt. 18:18).

Paul seems a reasonable role model in this respect. Even in terms of his earthly qualifications, he was a dual citizen – as Jewish as gefilte fish, yet a full Roman citizen from birth. Born in Tarsus, he was a world-traveller even before he became a Christian, having done advanced study in Jerusalem under the Pharisee and teacher of the law, Gamaliel. Paul was a global citizen, conscious of his own culture(s) through exposure to others. Yet he had a clear identity of his own. He was able to cope with different cultures and to use them to serve God (1 Cor 9:20–22). One of the most interesting of his mission visits in this regard was his brief stay in the university city of Athens (Acts 17:16–34). Athens was a city beyond its prime but still retained a grand reputation and a distinct culture. Paul knew quite a bit about that culture and used his knowledge to participate effectively in cultural exchanges with the city's inhabitants. But how did he do this? And how should we modify our approach to a culture or subculture based on our knowledge and appreciation of it?

Spreading the gospel to other cultures has often meant spreading Western European or American social customs and values, even clothing.

> Your satellite can reach that Eskimo,
>   He wears a suit and tie;
> Restyles his hair like girls from Tupelo
>   And sings 'Sweet Bye and Bye';
> He's meeting all your strange requirements,
>   He thinks you can't be fooled;
> He'll get the rules and laws and sacraments
>   By sending cheques to you.

> Terry Taylor, 'Return of the Beat Menace'
> on DA's *Darn Floor, Big Bite* (Frontline Records, 1988)

On the other hand, some have advocated complete immersion within a culture, so that Christians communicate as the culture communicates and as far as possible hold to the same methods and values. The goal is to blend in until the *only* thing distinctive about you is the gospel. Paul didn't fall for either of these extremes, although what he wound up doing was no less extreme in its own way.

But first things first. What do we mean by culture? Is it a simple set of equations: cultured = Stravinsky; barbaric = Satriani? It's not that easy. For the purposes of this chapter, we understand culture to be the creative work by which a people-group arrange and see the basic materials of their surroundings in a pattern that sustains them in their community life. It's almost as if every element in that pattern carries the societal DNA of their distinctive beliefs and values. The Chinese Mandarin's long sleeves and even longer fingernails indicated his class, his scholarly occupation and his freedom from 'demeaning' manual labour. Western male rock musicians of a certain vintage preserve long hair and long fingernails symbolic of other preoccupations and values!

Seeing the world through someone else's eyes will alter profoundly our own perceptions.

When we are inside it, our culture becomes for us the glasses through which we see the world around us. The trouble is, we forget we're wearing them. We forget we had to learn those beliefs and customs, and we assume that they are inherent, that they come with the genes. We assume that we are seeing clearly what is really out there. Our culture's lifestyle and customs give us purpose and meaning. They make us different from, maybe better than, 'them'. All of this brings a sense of community and of identity. To us, our patterns of belief and custom are 'right' and normal, and provide us with a sense of security. But, as with putting on someone else's glasses, immersion in a different culture will almost certainly cause blurs, disorientation and headaches. When you don another's glasses, far from forgetting them, they dominate your perception. Seeing the world through someone else's eyes will alter profoundly our own perceptions.

For most Christians, the first step towards confronting culture will be simply noticing that we, like all human beings, live in a culture. Once we know that, we can move on to discover more about it.

Being interested

Learning to become more interested in culture sounds like odd advice to give a Christian. Many of us were brought up in churches in which we were taught to keep away from the world and its ways. But communicating the gospel still entails communication, and part of any communication is knowing the people to whom you are communicating: knowing what their culture makes easy for them to believe and what it makes difficult.

It is something of a surprise to Christians today that when Paul gave his speech to the Athenians on Mars Hill, he did not quote scripture to them.

It is something of a surprise to Christians today that when Paul gave his speech to the Athenians on Mars Hill (Acts 17:22–31), he did not quote Old Testament scripture to them. Instead, remarkably, he quoted something he had spotted as he walked around their city: a dedication inscribed on one of their idols (17:23). This was a deliberate decision on his part. When Paul spoke to Jews, he often quoted the scriptures (cf. 13:13–43): they were familiar to that audience and would be heard with respect. However, when explaining the gospel in Athens, Paul referred instead to matters that *the Athenians* knew and respected: not only to the inscription but also to some passages from their own pagan poets (17:28), authors with whom Paul himself disagreed on very basic issues.

But how did he know their writings so well as to be able to quote them? Why would he run the risk of seeming to endorse their paganism? You can be sure that Paul's 'preparation' included much prayer and reading of scripture, but he also became interested in the *culture* of his hearers, and this interest helped him to communicate effectively within it. We can't be certain how Paul went about obtaining his background knowledge. It is difficult to imagine him trotting into the local Athenian public library and obtaining a visitor's short-term pass so that he could photocopy scrolls of recent Epicurean philosophy. On the other hand, it seems to be more than simply that he acquired his knowledge of these things by virtue of being a citizen of an Hellenised empire.

True communication has as much to do with personality, attitude and a host of other factors.

It is sometimes argued that Paul knew these pagan writings because his rabbinic training included the study of pamphlets that quoted and then refuted paganism. This may be so, but it is not the only way he came to know the cultures he encountered. In his writings, Paul sometimes used images of the Games: for example, in his letter to Corinth, where the Isthmian Games rivalled the Olympics (1 Cor 9:20–27). He surely did not glean *that* information from propaganda pamphlets. It seems much more likely that Paul found out about people because he really liked them, loved them even, and was naturally curious about their interests and backgrounds. And he did not use this knowledge in a utilitarian way, simply to convert them: rather, he just wanted to be with them, and it was this that made him a good communicator of the gospel.

We are all called to communicate the gospel. Insofar as that entails communication, it entails knowing something about the culture into which we are communicating and being willing to 'get alongside' it. 'Getting alongside' may involve learning to think outside of our own cultural boxes and entering into the thought-world of another culture. 'Getting alongside' may involve choosing to move away from our own culture towards others. However, it also implies that there is some distance between the two.

An evangelist can, up to a point, get away with the view that 'communication = words' but this is a very modern, Western point of view. For most people, true communication has as much to do with personality, attitude and a host of other factors. Equal to, or even more important than, the words we say is the persona we project to others. So when Paul claimed, 'I became a Gentile to win the Gentiles', he had in mind something deeper and wider than merely being conversant with his audience's intellectual and philosophical heritage and aesthetics. One assumes that, in his friendship and discipling of non-Jews, he adopted those of their customs and values which did not contradict the gospel. After visiting some cities he would moved on quickly,

For most of us, prophecy currently happens inside the church.

while in others he stayed for months or years. Those longer periods would increasingly have involved him in biculturalism with all its struggles, and probably contributed to his being not entirely accepted by his fellow Jews, always seeming a bit 'foreign' to the locals (as in Ephesus, Acts 19).

Getting real: expert knowledge or credibility?

It is difficult to see how we can really reach a culture without knowing it. But, whether we are communicating to another culture or to our own, our goal should not be to become so expert as to impress those around us with our great learning. Rather, our goal is to live in the same world in the same century – something that is vital to our credibility. It is extremely easy for others to dismiss the message about Jesus if it looks and sounds as though the person delivering it still lives in the 1900s. Besides learning to communicate in the language and idioms of our listeners, we are also communicating that we know what's really going on and are not just clinging to the gospel because we are ignorant of alternative viewpoints. It's not unusual, for instance, for some Christians to think that the only reason for knowing anything at all about science is to allow them to speak as an expert in favour of creationism against evolution. But we have all seen how people regard any expert with whom they do not agree. Being an expert is no guarantee of success, and being a self-educated expert with a diver-

It's not unusual... for some Christians to think that the only reason for knowing anything at all about science is to allow them to speak as an expert in favour of creationism against evolution.

gent opinion is probably as good a recipe for failure as you'll find anywhere.

In his references to the Athenians' statues and poets, Paul seems to portray himself not as an expert on their culture but as an interested party, an attentive tourist. No one would award him a postgraduate degree for his knowledge, but it is clear that his audience could not simply maintain that he was a fossil with his head in the sand (a fossil of an ostrich?). Their initial caricature of him was as a 'picker of seeds' (Acts 17:18): this has been translated as 'babbler' in the NIV – most likely a characterisation of him as someone who picks up ideas from here and there but who does not understand them all that well.

Generally, we communicate best when the people to whom we are talking feel that we know about the same amount as they do. If they think that they know a lot more about things, you're in trouble: why should they listen to *you*, unless you're asking questions? But if they are made to feel as though you know a lot more than they do, you're in trouble again: they will want to find holes in the 'so-called expert's armour'. You can see this happening when Christians argue about creationism or politics or Sunday shopping: an approach that says, 'I can prove ...', brings out the worst in the person on the street, whereas an approach that says, 'You know what I've never understood about...?', yields greater sympathy. We needn't come across as experts in order to be credible. It's better to be interested and curious than to be an all-knowing curiosity.

It's better to be interested and curious than to be an all-knowing curiosity.

Staying focused

It is true that the Christian who learns to regard other people as more than potential trophies, who learns to be interested in them and their culture for their own sakes, always faces the risk of 'going native'. Paul never lost sight of his dual citizenship, nor did he ever forget which passport would ultimately matter. We know that we cannot serve two masters – we cannot serve God and mammon (Matt 6:24) – but we also know that seeking to serve God almost always entails acting *in* the world. We cannot really claim to love God, whom we have not seen, if we do not love our fellow human beings whom we have seen (1 John 4:20).

Some writers have made a fuss about the fact that it's not only references to the Old Testament that appear to be suppressed in the Athens speech. Nowhere in the speech (as we have it) does Paul mention the name of Jesus. Is he being 'politically correct' and watering down the biblical message? Is this a speech advocating that his hearers convert to Christianity, or merely that they become more enlightened idol worshippers?

Although Paul appeared to refer often to the Athenians' statues, temples and poets, in fact this was all aimed at teaching them something about the true God. Paul was leading naturally and irresistibly to their need to repent (Acts 17:30). As we will see later, there was no way that any but the most inattentive of Athenian listeners could have mistaken his speech for one that condoned Athenian religious practices.

It is worth noticing that although Paul did not mention the name of Jesus in the speech, the whole process of communication had begun with his speaking quite plainly about Jesus (17:18). In his initial contact with the Athenians in the marketplace, it seems that he had indeed preached to them of Jesus and the resurrection; but they seem to have understood him incorrectly as speaking about a god, Jesus, and his wife-god, Resurrection (a feminine noun in the Greek), and that is why they were accusing him of preaching 'foreign gods' in the plural. This would explain the somewhat odd and angular content and shape of one part of his speech (17: 30–31): Paul was seeking to explain that Jesus was not another mythical god off in some fairytale land called Olympus: rather, he was a man who had lived on the earth and whom the Creator God had appointed. And 'resurrection' was not some goddess, but the actual raising of people from the dead. Paul demonstrated that he understood that his hearers' misunderstandings had arisen out of their cultural background, and that he was able to address them.

As an aside, it is interesting to note that when Paul went to Corinth, another Greek city, his tactics were quite different. Athens was an ancient university city, whose history stretched back to the golden days of Greece and philosophy. But Corinth was a totally new city, a Roman colony and commercial shipping centre, rebuilt upon the rubble of ancient Corinth which had been destroyed by Rome and which had remained virtually unoccupied for a whole century. The Corinthian culture was very different from that of Athens, and the Corinthians' taste for eloquence and learning was little more than a pretentious veneer. Paul clearly knew that they wanted to be seen as appreciating eloquence, and he regarded himself as being able

Paul was seeking to explain that Jesus was not another mythical god off in some fairytale land called Olympus.

to deliver it. Yet, because he recognised their vanity, he decided *not* to approach the Corinthians with eloquent words but to teach nothing but Christ crucified (1 Cor 2:1–2).

Confronting culture

The amazing thing about Paul's work both in Corinth and in Athens was the way that he refused to use his knowledge of their cultures merely to flatter them, to give them what they *wanted* to hear or to discuss how much they had in common. He was emphatically not saying to them, 'You Athenians and we Christians agree on so much; therefore you should accept and appreciate Christ as I have accepted and appreciated your religion.' A modern reader might feel this is what Paul has done, but you have only to place yourself in the Athenians' position to feel the speech very differently.

Quite the reverse is true: Paul used his knowledge of their values and their writings to try to convince them that they were *wrong* and, in fact, they should *already* have known that they were wrong. His speech in Athens was more of a confrontation than a walking arm-in-arm.

First, appearing before a group of academic philosophers in the leading intellectual centre of the ancient world, Paul focused precisely on what they were *ignorant* about – the god of which they admitted ignorance (Acts 17:23). If Paul praised the Athenians for having such an idol, it was not the idol he was praising but, rather, their admission of ignorance. Needless to say, this group of philosophers (literally 'lovers of wisdom') would have felt somewhat uncomfortable about a talk which had as its subject the gaps in their knowledge. And Paul returned to this theme of their ignorance when he opens the second half of the speech: 'In the past God overlooked such ignorance...' (v 30). Only by appreciating the character of your audience can you tailor such an exquisite put-down.

Second, Paul knows enough about the Athenians' idol worship to be able to detail how it was ignorant. He provided them with what amounts to a checklist of wrong-headedness: you Athenians admit ignorance about the identity of God (v 23); you are wrong about where a god would live (v 24); you are wrong about how a god would want to be served (v 25); you are wrong about gods being localised and how to look for them (vs 26–27); and you are wrong about how they can be represented (vs 28–29).

Third, Paul anticipated their objections. When he returned to the theme of their ignorance in verse 30, it is not, as some think, a matter of him finding the answer to the modern question of how God regards people who haven't heard the gospel; rather, Paul's response is rooted directly in first-century culture and religious understanding.

Ancient religion operated on the principle of *pax deorum*, peace with the gods. People went out of their way not to offend the gods; they sought to worship them properly and to fulfil all vows to the letter, because to give offence to the gods was to invite trouble – plagues, earthquakes and other disasters. Although this was not exactly how his Judaism operated, Paul knew how his pagan audience would be thinking: "How can our religion be so wrong, since there are no horrible plagues?" He anticipated their viewpoint well enough to know some of the questions they would be asking.

Paul anticipated his audience's misunderstandings because he understood their culture and their way of thinking, but he did not use this awareness to try to convince the Athenians that he was just like them and that Christianity was only a short hop from where they already stood. Instead, he actually sharpened the differences between their world-view and his, in the process implicitly criticising them by referring to the ignorance of these 'lovers of wisdom'.

Yet it was a measured response compared with his initial feelings (v 16). To forge the link with his audience, Paul reined in his repulsion and deep distress about their idols enough to transmute it into an ambiguous, almost complimentary comment. He begins his speech as a 'cultural tourist' before moving on to identify with their culture, switching from the second person plural ('*you* are very religious ... *your* objects of worship ... what *you* worship as something unknown ... *your* own poets') to the first person plural ('he is not far from each of *us* ... since *we* are his offspring...'). No longer is he thinking purely in terms of 'us and them' but 'we': the shared human experience denied by the teaching of racial or religious superiority, of which the Athenians could be as guilty as the most separatist of the Jews. This is no public relations attempt to establish a sense of commonality but, rather, a deeply-held conviction – the mystery to which the Pharisee Saul was converted – that the Messiah sent by God was for the Gentiles also.

Like Paul, all Christians are citizens of two cultures. Like him, we must seek to understand, to anticipate and to get alongside those whom we are addressing. But we

No longer is he thinking purely in terms of 'us and them' but 'we': the shared human experience.

must do so not in a false way and not merely to feel like we belong to their culture. Instead we should seek to sharpen the distinctions between our faith and any culture, and to point all cultures toward the God who is the Lord of all nations and eras.

> '... he made all the nations, that they should inhabit the whole earth...'
>
> *(Acts 17:26)*

Chapter 2

Presenting the challenge: Christ and culture

Tony Lane

How should Christians relate to the world? How should the church relate to society? Should Christians as individuals, or the church as a body, be involved in politics?

These are all important, practical issues that the church has had to face from the beginning of its existence, and, over the ages, Christians have taken a variety of stances in response to these questions. In 1952, in his classic work *Christ and Culture*, Richard Niebuhr expounded five basic Christian positions in relation to the world.[1] His analysis has met with a certain amount of criticism, but his account of the five positions has proved very helpful and is still used today. In this chapter we will follow his basic analysis, though there will be a certain amount of adaptation in its application to understanding the relation between Christ and culture. As we do so, we will ask four questions of the five basic positions:

How do they understand sin?
What is the church?
How do Christians relate to the non-Christian world?
What attitude should Christians have to politics?

This last question will be illustrated by the attitude Christians have to their national flag, a helpful test case.

We are considering five basic positions: can we assume, therefore, that one is right and the other four are wrong? Not necessarily. In the New Testament we find contrasting assessments of the state in two quite different books:

> Everyone must submit himself to the governing authorities, for there is no authority except that which God has established. The authorities that exist have been established by God. Consequently, he who rebels against the authority is rebelling against what God has instituted, and those who do so will bring judgment on themselves. For rulers hold no terror for those who do right, but for those who do wrong. Do you want to be free from fear of the one in authority? Then do what is right and he will commend you. For he is God's servant to do you good. But if you do wrong, be afraid, for he does not bear the sword for nothing. He is God's servant, an agent of wrath to bring punishment on the wrongdoer. Therefore, it is necessary to submit to the authorities, not only because of possible punishment but also because of conscience.
> **(Romans 13:1–5)**

> And the dragon stood on the shore of the sea. And I saw a beast coming out of the sea. He had ten horns and seven heads, with ten crowns on his horns, and on each head a blasphemous name. The beast I saw resembled a leopard, but had feet like those of a bear and a mouth like that of a lion. The dragon gave the beast his power and his throne and great authority. One of the heads of the beast seemed to have had a fatal wound, but the fatal wound had been healed. The whole world was astonished and followed the beast. Men worshipped the dragon because he had given authority to the beast, and they also worshipped the beast and asked, 'Who is like the beast? Who can make war against him?'

The beast was given a mouth to utter proud words and blasphemies and to exercise his authority for forty-two months. He opened his mouth to blaspheme God, and to slander his name and his dwelling-place and those who live in heaven. He was given power to make war against the saints and to conquer them. And he was given authority over every tribe, people, language and nation.
(Revelation 13:1–7)

These passages present very different perspectives, but both are part of Christian revelation. To some extent they may be said to apply to the state in differing circumstances, but it is also true that they both apply, in varying degrees, to all manifestations of the state. They represent the two sides of the Christian response to the state. To hold to one alone without the other would be to lose the balance espoused in the New Testament. We will find that all five positions expounded by Niebuhr are able to cite biblical passages in their support. The question to be asked of them is not how many texts they can cite, but how well they succeed in holding in balance the different strands of biblical teaching.

Finally, it is not being suggested that all Christians today, or at any time in history, have fitted neatly into one or other of these five categories. These are *basic positions*. Many Christians will hold intermediate views, whether out of considered conviction or (more often) because they have failed to think through the issues.

1 Christ against culture

The first position involves rejection of the world, a stance that is found in much early monasticism, for example, and in more 'sectarian' forms of Protestantism.[2]

This attitude to the world was manifested in the sixteenth-century Radical Reformation (by the Anabaptists) and is seen today in an extreme form in a similar group, the Amish in Pennsylvania. It was also manifest among some of the early Brethren in the nineteenth century, and is found among the Jehovah's Witnesses.

This position is based upon a radical view of the sinfulness of the world which is seen as being in opposition to God. This is in contrast to the church which is the pure Bride of Christ. Christians are expected to be radically different to unbelievers, and their lives are to be pure and holy. Groups holding to this position are liable to hold perfectionist views, believing that it is possible for Christians to be totally purified from sin. There is no room for the idea of a 'mixed' church comprising saints and sinners. The church *is* the company of saints and should remain separate: 'Do not be yoked together with unbelievers... "come out from them and be separate, says the Lord" ' (2 Cor 6:14,17).

Those who hold to this view are likely to discourage believers from participating in the secular world, whether this involves going down to the pub, joining the Rotary Club or going to the theatre. The Christian's contact with non-Christians should be confined to necessary activities such as employment and trade, apart from the specific goal of evangelism. As regards politics, such groups generally have no interest in secular politics or government: such involvement is to be shunned by believers. The state is liable to be seen in terms of the book of Revelation (as the beast from the sea, 13:1–10; or as

Those holding to this position have tended to shun the world, as did the earliest monks.

Babylon, chapters 17–18). There will be little, if any, sense of loyalty to the national flag, and many such Christians will be pacifists. Some, such as a near neighbour of mine, will even maintain that the Christian ought not to vote. The social implications of the gospel are seen in terms of its effects in the church and not in terms of its impact on godless society at large.

What are the pros and cons of this position? On the positive side, it clearly takes seriously at least part of the teaching of the New Testament, such as the call to Christians to be separate, distinctive and holy. High standards are set for the church, which is seen as the light of the world (Matt 5:14–16). Those holding to this position have tended to shun the world, as did the earliest monks in a very literal fashion; yet, in the long term, they have often indirectly influenced that world.

On the negative side, this view of sin, though radical, is also superficial and inadequate. The world is steeped in sin, but all of church history shows that escaping from sin is not as simple as leaving the world. Sin is the enemy *within*, even for Christians. The history of sectarian groups amply illustrates this point. Their idealistic view of the converted Christian has tended to blind them to the fact of their own capacity to sin and has thus made them all the more vulnerable to the danger.

Another problem with this position is that it is based upon a weak doctrine of creation. The world is correctly seen as sinful, but it is forgotten that the world is also God's creation. The world is not pure evil but, rather, something good that has become corrupted.

This position's superficial view of sin easily leads to petty legalism: the Amish, for example, use hooks rather than buttons because the latter imply pride. Moving closer to home, some Christians give the impression that the essence of being a Christian is avoiding certain 'worldly' activities. Such legalisms trivialise sin and undermine the gospel.

Finally, it is just not possible to escape a culture simply by physical and social withdrawal. It has been aptly commented that in the age of videos and the Internet, it is only too easy for Christians to reverse Jesus' dictum (John 17:14–15) and to be of the world without being *in* it.

2 The Christ of culture

This second position is the opposite of the first and is sometimes called 'Culture Christianity'. Christianity is all but identified with a particular culture, so much so that there is no significant tension between them. This has often manifested itself as 'national religion', and has recently been seen in a very negative light in Eastern Europe, in the identification of Croat national identity with Catholicism, and Serb national identity with Orthodoxy. More positively, this identification can help to preserve national identity from assault, as with Polish Catholicism against the twin onslaughts of German Nazism and Russian Communism. Closer to home, one thinks of those who have identified Christianity with socialism, those who sing 'Jerusalem' at Conservative party conferences or who identify Christianity with British middle-class values. While the first position (*Christ against culture*) is held by a minority of evangelicals, there would be few if any who would espouse this second position.

What view of sin is held? Sin is regarded as dangerous,

but is something that can be overcome and is not universal. The radical sinfulness of humanity is viewed as a bizarre notion. The church provides a religious seal and validation for nationalism, socialism or middle-class values. The good Christian will be the good patriot, socialist or bourgeois. Christianity provides a religious sanction for the values of society and does not seriously challenge them. The church will be involved in, and publicly committed to, society. One would expect to find the national flag, and maybe even military emblems, flying beside the cross, and probably also a memorial portraying the war dead as Christian martyrs.

This position is not without its merits. The world is seen as God's good creation, and it is recognised that God is at work in human society. The church is involved in society, and affirms and validates what is good in the social order. However, on the negative side, there is a low view of sin, which is all too easily located in the rival nation or political ideology, and there is a failure of the gospel to challenge one's own society or ideology. The Christian faith has become subservient to another agenda.

The two positions reviewed thus far, *Christ against culture* and *the Christ of culture*, are extreme. They involve simply rejecting or affirming culture on the basis of a one-sided appeal to the doctrine of sin or creation. The following two positions are more refined and qualified versions of the above.

3 Christ above culture

This is a more refined version of the previous position, *the Christ of culture*. It involves *adding* Christ to culture, a two-tiered approach. The two tiers are often described as 'Nature' and 'Grace'. 'Nature' – human culture and reason – is accepted more or less without question, and regarded as part of God's 'general revelation'. The purpose of the Christian faith is not fundamentally to challenge 'Nature', though there may be specific evils in society which need correcting. The distinctive role of the Christian faith is to add an extra dimension, a second level, which is God's special revelation. In other words, this position involves accepting culture and society more or less as they are and adding a Christian dimension to them. This view is often traced back to Thomas Aquinas, and is found among Protestants who are relatively uncritical of culture, including a minority of evangelicals.

Sin is regarded as universal, and all are in need of salvation, but society and culture are fundamentally good and are not significantly spoiled by sin. The fall may affect the human *will*, but not, in the main, human reason. The church's role is to affirm culture, society and the state. Salvation and 'religion' are provided by the church as an added dimension over and above human culture, but Christians do not seriously challenge the social and intellectual achievements of the world.

According to this position, the Christian will be a model citizen – indeed, he or she will follow higher moral precepts which go above and beyond what is expected of the model citizen. The expectation is that the Christian will go beyond the morality of society but not normally against it. Government and the political order are ordained by God and are based upon 'natural' (as opposed to 'revealed') morality (Rom 13:1–7). Christians will feel positively about their nation's flag but will not confuse it with the essence of their faith.

This position is in many ways superior to those we have considered so far. It relates the Christian faith to society and culture, and enables a constructive Christian engagement in them. Its most serious weakness is that it is based on too optimistic a view of natural law, of a universal moral law independent of Christian revelation. It may have worked reasonably well at a time when society at large accepted the Christian moral vision, when 'natural law' was almost identical to the Ten Commandments. However, as we become an increasingly secular society, where less and less credence is given to a Christian world-view, it is becoming apparent that there is no strictly neutral 'natural law'. When society turns its back on Christianity, 'natural law' becomes non-Christian if not anti-Christian. An approach to society founded on the premise that 'natural law' is a neutral basis on which to build Christian ethics is becoming increasingly out of place in today's world. Those Christians who work from this position will find themselves accepting concepts of freedom or 'human rights' which originate out of an anti-Christian world-view. The fundamental weakness of this position is that, like the more extreme position *the Christ of culture*, it emphasises the doctrine of creation but neglects the doctrine of sin.

4 Christ in tension with culture

This is a more refined version of the first position, *Christ against culture*, like it placing greater emphasis on sin than on creation. The Reformer, Martin Luther, is a classic exponent and, more recently, it has been very popular in the evangelical tradition.[3] While the basic framework for *Christ above culture* is that of Nature–Grace, for *Christ in tension with culture* the framework is Sin–Grace. We see here the same contrast as between *the Christ of Culture* and *Christ against Culture*, albeit in a more muted form. Here 'Christ' is held in tension with 'culture' rather than simply rejecting it.

This stance holds a radical view of sin similar to that of *Christ against culture*, but here it is taken further. We are *all* sinners and *every* area of human activity is affected by sin. All human society is sinful, including *Christian* society, the church. The world is indeed sinful, but there is no simple escape through overt separation from it. The church is a mixed body, not the pure company of the saints. Who among the congregation of professing Christians is a genuine Christian is known only to God. In that sense, the true church is 'invisible': not that it has no institutional expression, but that the *boundaries* of the church – who is a real Christian and who is not – are known only to God. This view of the church clearly provides a rationale for the inclusive state church, which embraces most of society and includes nominal as well as genuine Christians. But the analysis offered applies equally to the 'gathered church', to the congregation composed only of those claiming to be genuine believers.

Christian distinctiveness lies not in overt separation from the world but in a distinctive lifestyle lived *in* the world. Emphasis on separation can easily lead to petty legalisms, where the mark of the true Christian is obedience to rules relating to smoking, drinking, clothes, and so on (Matt 23:23–24). However, the distinctive mark of the true Christian lies not in externals like these, but in such things as inner motivation and especially love. Government and politics are good and ordained by God (Rom 13:1–7; 1 Pet 2:13–14), and it is our Christian duty to obey and to serve the 'powers that be': as Luther put it, if there is a shortage of hangmen and you are qualified, you should offer your services![4] But the state has a strictly limited role to play: that of restraining sin and keeping anarchy at bay by preserving law and order (Rom 13:4; 1 Tim 2:1–2). The Christian will profess loyalty to the national flag, but there will be no temptation to view it as a 'Christian' flag.

Luther taught that there are two 'kingdoms' or 'realms': there is the *spiritual* realm involving issues of eternal life and salvation, which are the concerns of the church; and there is the *temporal* realm involving the issues of this world, such as politics and economics. The latter are the concerns of secular government. The temporal realm is to be managed on the basis not of the gospel or of Christian revelation but of 'natural law'. The goal of the Christian in society is primarily negative (to preserve law and order) rather than utopian (to bring in the kingdom of God).

There are many positive features about this position: it is based upon a realistic view of human nature and sin; there are realistic expectations about what can be expected from politicians; and it avoids confusion of the two realms. Too often in the past the gospel has been turned into an ephemeral political message. In the Victorian era, Welsh Nonconformity became closely identified with the emerging trade union and Labour movements. The eventual outcome? Wales became a bastion for trade unionism and the Labour Party, and the chapels went into catastrophic decline. It would be too simplistic to see a simple 'cause and effect' here, but it would be hard to deny any connection between the two events.

On the negative side, this position can, like the more extreme *Christ against culture*, be faulted for emphasising the doctrine of sin but neglecting the doctrine of creation. It also falls into the same trap as *Christ above culture* in supposing that the secular realm can be based upon some neutral 'natural law'. Nazism was the wake-up call to the church on this issue, and now that we are awake we can see through the more benign, but equally threatening, influence of pagan 'natural law' in Western society today. No longer can we naively assume, as could Luther, that 'natural law' is roughly equivalent to the Ten Commandments, confronted as we are by a secular society that, far from being ideologically neutral, is becoming increasingly non-Christian and, indeed, anti-Christian. One of the tragedies of the Nazi era was that the Lutheran attitude helped to persuade many (not all) in the German church to accept Nazism passively. Freeing the secular realm from Christian restraints has proved to be too dangerous.

There is no pure church guaranteed to contain only genuine Christians.

These days there are very few Christian theologians who would be willing to accept the idea that politics is a no-go area for the church and theology. Such an idea would find more favour with politicians: it was, and is, the only terms under which Communist governments are prepared to deal with the church. At the opposite end, some Conservative politicians have defended the secular–religious divide as a way of protecting themselves from 'meddling clergy'.

5 Christ transforming culture

The final position is in some ways a development of the previous one. The Christian faith is not just *in tension* with culture but has a role to play in *transforming* it. This is the traditional Reformed approach:[5] The basic framework is not Nature–Grace (that of *Christ above culture*) nor Sin–Grace (that of *Christ in tension with culture*) but Creation–Fall–Redemption, thus taking into full account both creation and sin. The cross is taken seriously (as with *Christ in tension with culture*) but the incarnation is also emphasised (as with *Christ above culture*). God has entered into and become involved with human society and culture.

> There never has been, and in this age never will be, a pacifist government.

This position holds a radical view of sin (as with *Christ in tension with culture*) but there is more room for emphasis on the goodness of God's creation. Human culture is not evil in itself but, rather, is something good that has been spoiled or corrupted. Society is to be seen not merely as a just order for the corrupt but as a good order corrupted. Human culture is indeed sinful and under the judgement of God; but since God is also sovereign and active in history, improvement is possible. The church is a mixed body, not the pure company of the saints (as with *Christ in tension with culture*). There is no pure church guaranteed to contain only genuine Christians, and neither is the church perfect; but it is possible to reform the church and to make it less imperfect.

Christian distinctiveness lies not in overt separation from the world but in a distinctive lifestyle lived in the world (as with *Christ in tension with culture*). However, politics and government play a more positive role – that of bringing about God's rule rather than merely preserving law and order. Christian vocation includes not just evangelism and church work but also the call to be involved in society, whether in politics, economics, arts or the media. Believers should be seeking to bring a Christian influence into all of these areas and to be making the gospel visible there. Those holding to this position will normally profess loyalty to their national flag, though they may, in extreme and revolutionary circumstances, work towards changing that flag.

On the positive side, those holding this position have brought profound changes to society: for example, it was Reformed rather than Lutheran Protestantism that (for good or ill) provided the cradle for capitalism and democracy. The Dutch, English and American revolutions have profoundly affected the course of history. The history of Christian social reforms in the last two hundred years is an honourable one.

However, on the negative side, one outcome of this view has been the use of military force and other worldly weapons in the name of the gospel. The Cromwellian era left some bitter memories, for example, in Ireland. Recent Anabaptist social thought offers an alternative model for transforming culture which is based on non-violence; but while this may serve as a model for a pressure group, or possibly an opposition party, it provides no model for government. There never has been, and in this age never will be, a pacifist government. While it may be possible to run one's foreign policy on a non-violent basis, this is not an option open to the police force or the Inland Revenue. Ultimately, the Anabaptist policy remains that of separation from the actual process of government, although groups holding to it may have influence as pressure groups. In rare instances non-violent protest can bring down a regime, but it is never possible to replace it with a pacifist government. At the *strategic* level though, a pacifist, countercultural political strategy may be the most effective one for a Christian minority in the present post-Constantinian West.

Other fears concerning *Christ transforming culture* have proved true enough. So desperate is the contemporary church to avoid the mistakes made under the Nazis, there is a determination to locate injustice, oppression and worse in the most benign of regimes. The boom in political theologies has led to just the confusion of the gospel with secular programmes that Luther feared. One example will suffice: Jürgen Moltmann, perhaps the best-known living Reformed theologian, has throughout his literary career, devoted considerable effort into unfolding the socio-political outworkings of the Christian faith. And what has been the outcome? In the 1960s he espoused a theology of revolution; in the 1970s he espoused the Democratic Socialism of the SPD (German Socialist Party); in the 1980s he threw in his lot with the Greens; and, more recently, he has espoused an anti-hierarchical feminism. Is this really evidence of a deepening engagement with the biblical revelation? Or is it a good indication of the development of secular, left-of-centre progressive thought in Germany during those decades, whether one considers this to be a good or a bad development?

A personal postscript

Having set out the five different positions, I will conclude with a personal assessment of how we might resolve this issue today, using the test case of Christian involvement in politics.

The line that Christians should opt out of politics and leave it to the ungodly (*Christ against culture*) is simply irresponsible. In the Old Testament, Daniel is a role model for the godly politician fully involved in a non-Christian society. Those who urge Christians to opt out should recognise that they are condemning Wilberforce for his efforts to end the slave trade. On the other hand, there is no great value in Christians being involved if they are going to equate Christianity with an alien ideology, be this socialism, capitalism or nationalism (*the Christ of culture*). Nor is the situation much improved if they accept uncritically a secular political ideology and see the Christian message as merely adding a spiritual dimension over and above it (*Christ above culture*). As secular Western ideologies become increasingly anti-Christian, the weakness of those two positions will become more and more apparent.

For similar reasons, it is also unacceptable to say that the church should stick to religion and leave politics to the state (*Christ in tension with culture*). Christ is Lord over the whole of life, not just over the 'religious' side of life. He is Lord at 11 o'clock on Monday morning as well as 11 o'clock on Sunday morning. If Christians are to be involved in politics, theirs must be a *Christian* voice. This is far, far more easily said than done. In the days of party politics, room for dissenting personal conviction is limited. Christian involvement in politics is not about proclaiming, like Elijah, 'I am the only one left' (1 Kings 19:10); rather, it is about reaching principled compromises to achieve practical results. The task is made no easier when the majority of 'political theology' on offer is little more than contemporary (or recent) secular ideologies with a thin religious veneer.

The Christian who is involved in politics may view the position espoused by *Christ transforming culture* as a noble ideal; however, experience proves that it easily lapses into being too accommodating (*the Christ of culture*) or unchallenging (*Christ above culture*). So, if our aim is to transform the world in which we live, we constantly need to be challenged by the insights of *Christ in tension with culture* – not feeling too 'at home' in society; being 'in the world but not of it'.

Endnotes

1   H Richard Niebuhr, *Christ and Culture*, Faber & Faber, 1952. A brief exposition of Niebuhr's view is found in his previously unpublished paper, 'Types of Christian ethics', in Glen Harold Stassen *et al*, *Authentic Transformation: A New Vision of Christ and Culture*, Abingdon, 1996, pp15–29. This is followed in the same book by John Howard Yoder, '*How H. Richard Niebuhr reasoned: A critique of Christ and Culture*', pp31–89.

2   The word 'sectarian' here is not a value judgement and does not imply heresy; rather, it serves as a sociological term referring to a particular view of the church as a radically distinctive group of people, separate from society and withdrawn from the world.

3   R Kolb, 'Niebuhr's "Christ and Culture in Paradox" revisited,' *Lutheran Quarterly* 10 (1996) pp259–79, criticises Niebuhr's exposition of Luther and offers a more positive appreciation of this position.

4   Martin Luther, 'Temporal authority: To what extent it
     should be obeyed' in *Luther's Works*, Muhlenberg Press,
     1962, vol 45, p95.

5   Charles Scriven, *The Transformation of Culture: Christian
     Social Ethics after H. Richard Niebuhr*, Herald Press, 1988,
     pp17–29, criticises Niebuhr for relegating the Anabaptists
     to the Christ against Culture position. He argues that there
     is a more valid Anabaptist model for the transformation of
     culture (eg pp20,26–32,146–58,167–94). However, the
     development of Anabaptist social thought since Niebuhr's
     death does not invalidate his assessment of the sixteenth-
     century Anabaptists.

Chapter 3

The challenge of personhood: Towards a theology of personhood

Max Turner

What does it mean to be a 'person'?

We probably all have some fundamentally instinctive answer to that question. I am a person. You, the reader, are a person. It is clear, isn't it? But it may come as a surprise to learn that what it means to be a 'person' is actually a very controversial issue taking us right to the disputed heart of human existence.

Let us begin with a purely hypothetical and quite monstrous test case. Say we take a fertilised human ovum and put it in a very clever laboratory on a desert island. Our robotic laboratory is so clever it can simulate the mother's womb, birth, suckling, mucking-out and all the rest, including even perhaps some basic language teaching. Twenty-one years later, our fertilised egg has grown into an adult woman. She looks like any other woman on the planet but she has not had any contact with anyone else, not even with God (we have set up the experiment with his cooperation): he has agreed not to address her in any way. Would this woman – let's call her Jane (though she doesn't actually have any use for a name) – would Jane be a 'person'? If so, in what sense? And when did she become one?

A relatively mainstream philosophical and theological answer would be: yes, Jane is a person and perhaps has always been so, even from the first day of the experiment. Some might suggest, however, that she only 'became' what we mean by a 'person' when she was expelled from the laboratory 'womb' and cut off from its placenta. Others still, might argue she only became a person when she had grown up enough to begin to analyse the world around her, to make her own decisions, even to reflect on her own existence. Yet others would argue that Jane – at the ripe age of twenty-one! – is still no more than an individual biological case of the genus *homo*. She may possess the *potential* to become what we normally mean by a 'person', but she has not yet achieved any real personhood: an individual only becomes a person as she or he relates to others. This view may imply, for example, that if I have a terrible accident that leaves me in a terminal coma, I may have *been* a person, but my still-living remains have effectively ceased to be such.

I hope you are beginning to see some of the complexities, and that they are real-life issues! Let us look now a little deeper at one of the historically most influential approaches to this question.

The main philosophical and intellectual tradition of the West

What follows is necessarily a great over-simplification, but here goes...

For Plato, human beings consisted of two quite separate natures: a material body and, housed within it, an immortal 'soul'. For him, it was the soul that was the important part: it came from the heavenly world and was the thinking essence of our personal being. For Plato, the physical matter of this world was an inferior sort of existence altogether compared with the *psyche* ('soul' or 'rational being'). Matter was even evil, and it impeded and compromised the purity and rationality of the soul. On his view, the body was not really necessary for 'life' at all but something of a hindrance; death liberated the soul from its prison and enabled it to return to its true and heavenly existence. Thus Plato's master, Socrates, was able fearlessly to swallow the hemlock his executioner had placed in his hand, assured that by death he would become the true philosopher. Plato would have no problem with Jane being a person, for the essence of personhood is rationality and this is guaranteed by the presence of her soul. It may be nice to have other people to relate to, but they are in no sense fundamental to Jane's existence as a person.

We may trace something like this (with substantial variations) as the dominant view of personhood from Plato to our own time. For Augustine, as we shall see, the essence of creation in God's image is the rational power of the human soul. With the Enlightenment, French philosopher René Descartes (1596–1650) gave foundational status to such a view of personhood in his central assertion, 'I think, therefore I am', which means: 'I'm not quite so sure about *your* existence, but I know that *I* exist because the real "me" is the thinking machine somewhere between my eyeballs, which has just had this clever thought…'

If you follow that line and push it, it means that my being a person has really got nothing *essentially* to do with you. I am entirely distinct from you (and, according to the theory of evolution, I am competing with you for my very survival). I was fully a human person before you came on the stage alongside me. You can affect me in the sense that you may cause me hurt or joy; but the 'me' that you affect is fully a person without you. We may set up a state, together, agreeing laws that prevent us inconveniencing each other for our mutual benefit (and Plato was certainly interested in society; his justly most famous work is his *Republic*). It is also possible that I will love you, and may even show great courage and self-sacrifice to benefit you, but it is still the fully formed distinct independent 'I' that will do this.

What we take to be our individual persona is nothing more than an illusion.

All this is, of course, the well-spring of individualism, and individualism is the dominant (Western!) philosophy of our age even if it shows itself in a wide variety of forms, from German idealism and British utilitarianism to the recent philosophical debates about whether a person is a mind or a body.[1]

There are, naturally, intellectual wild cards. Analyses in the disciplines of psychology and functionalist sociology have pushed in the opposite direction, implying that there is virtually no meaningful and willing interiority to the individual. What we *take* to be our individual persona is nothing more than an illusion. It is 'really' just the civil war between the libido, the id and the super-ego (so Freud). Or it is 'nothing more' than the ebb and flow through us of purely social forces, and we can make new sorts of people by drastic social intervention (eg by suppressing or killing off the bourgeois sector, as has been tried by various types of collectivism from Marx to Pol Pot).

Or, yet again, behaviourists may try to persuade us

that what we take to be our free rational powers of thought and decision-making are really nothing more than a succession of biologically predetermined brain 'states' or 'events': that is, all brain activity (including every kind of sensory perception, 'thinking' and emotion) is the fixed product of genetic, anatomical, physiological and environmental conditions. According to such a view, what we applaud as the most daring, independent and radical thinking of great minds may well ultimately be explained in terms of a minor tweak of genetics, combined with a diet perhaps rather rich in certain vitamins, and a cold season of weather.[2]

But 'individualisms' of one form or another reign in the West. Individualism is not merely the dominant philosophy but also our *culture*. It is perhaps neatly epitomised in Frank Sinatra's 'I did it my way' and in the films that glorify mega-tough loners like Rambo and Mad Max. Even Western theological anthropology stemming from Augustine (it is claimed) has followed roughly the same track. It has elucidated humanity made in God's image largely in terms of the *rational* powers of the soul (though what place this leaves for the humanity of people with mental disability might stir questions). Within this rationale, full personhood may be perceived as innate to human existence and essentially prior to and independent of relations to others. Correspondingly, in theology there is the propensity to explain trinitarian relations within God in defective forms of 'social Trinity' which verge on tritheism (ie there are three individual gods – Father, Son and Spirit – but, fortunately, they get on quite well!).

Theological reflection

Almost all agree that by far the most important starting point for theological reflection on this issue is Genesis 1–3.

1. In God's image (Gen 1:26-31)

According to Genesis 1, what distinguishes humans from animals is that humankind alone is made 'in God's image' and 'after his likeness'. But what precisely does it mean to be created 'in God's image'? Western theology (that is, the Roman Catholic Church and the Protestant Reformation) has put forward a variety of explanations.

- Is it that we are able to think rationally, make deliberate decisions and communicate them in various forms of 'speech' (including writing, physical gestures and other forms of body language)?
- Is it that we have a moral sense of right and wrong?
- Is it that we have authority in creation?
- Is it that we have a social nature?

Each of these (and combinations of them) has been defended. Most famously, Augustine saw the pattern of the Trinity imaged in the *individual's* mind, will and emotions. But perhaps these premises miss the heart of the matter. It is the fathers of the Eastern church who may offer the more helpful explanation. Let us go back to Genesis 1:26: 'Let us make man in our image, and after our likeness'. What did this verse mean to the Eastern fathers, and what view of personhood does it entail?

For the Eastern fathers (essentially the Cappadocians like Basil of Caesarea, Gregory of Nyssa and Gregory of Nazianzus – all flourishing around AD350 onwards), it would mean that *we are persons in the same way that the Father, the Son and the Spirit are persons.* Now, when we reflect on the nature of personhood in God, we at once recognise a completely different view of personhood from the individualism of the West (epitomised in, for example, the Mad Max films).[3] This has enormous implications for our view of humankind made in God's image. God as Father, Son and Spirit are not three rugged super-macho individuals who are each *separately* God, but who happen to get along together well. If that were the case, Muslims and Jews would be right to accuse us of denying that God is One. We would be preachers of *three* Gods, not one; of tritheism, not monotheism.

For the Western fathers, this danger of tritheism was avoided by the rather unhelpful device of saying the Father, Son and Spirit shared together some immutable divine *substance*, or 'nature'. In the East, the danger of tritheism was faced differently. The unity of God was seen to consist not so much in a hypothetical 'nature' ('substance') as in *the full communion of Divine Persons.* On Eastern understanding, what we *mean* by the word 'God' is the communion together of Divine Being as Father, Son and Spirit. Within this communion, God's distinct personhood as Father only exists *in and through his relationship to the Son,* and God's personhood as the Son only emerges *in and through his intimate relationship to the Father.* (I should add that some of the Western fathers inclined in the same direction; notably Hilary of Poitier and Richard of St Victor.)

I hope you can see that here personhood does not consist in being distinct and separate *before* relating together: personhood arises precisely *through being together in relation.* God as Father, Son and Spirit are eternally turned towards each other in total belonging-ness, total openness and total love. This is the image or likeness in which we are made. Genesis 1:27 may hint at this when it concludes: 'So God created man in his own image ... male *and* female he created them'.

2. Immortal 'souls' in Genesis 2?

In Genesis 2, we have a second telling of the creation story, bringing fresh perspectives. Unfortunately, this account has become the basis for a traditional misun-derstanding of the nature of humanity: it has often been taken to imply that God first made Adam's body out of mere earthly elements and then blew into it the all-important immortal 'soul' (a bit like locking a ghost inside a box). This view is clearly very much like Plato's, but that is no accident: it only came about by reading the passage with Platonic (more correctly, Neoplatonic) spectacles. Genesis 2:7 states that God breathed into Adam the 'breath of life' and, as a result, he became a 'living being'. Unfortunately, the word translated as 'living being' in the Greek version of the Bible – the version read by virtually all the church fathers – is *psyche*, and this was the very word Plato used for the immortal soul. Hence, much later, but guided by the fathers, the Authorised Version of the Bible (the most influential English translation) rendered Genesis 2:7 thus: 'And the Lord God formed man of the dust of the ground, and breathed into his nostrils the breath of life; and man became a living soul.' This translation has led to the widespread view that God puts the real immortal person into the merely physical body at conception. It results, however, in a double misunderstanding.

First, there is nothing immortal about the 'living being' that God creates: quite the opposite. The Genesis account tells us that Adam and Eve would only *become* immortal if they were to eat from the tree of life – and that is the tree from whose presence they are exiled after the fall, lest they eat of it and live for ever (Gen 3:22–23).

Second, what is 'breathed into' Adam is not his personhood but simply 'vitality' or 'life'. If anything, we could put it the other way round and say that God created the *person* Adam out of the elements and then vivified it, brought it into life. This too would be a distortion, but a far milder one than the Platonic reading supposes.

Genesis 2 offers no support for the view that the essence of the person is something God implants in the otherwise foreign, physical 'soil' of the human body: rather, humans are vivified *bodies*. Genesis 2 offers no support to the (quite catholic) idea that the essential 'person' is some ontic 'being' which God attaches to the embryo.

3. Personhood in human beings created in God's image

One of the more helpful recent works on this theme is *The call to personhood* by Alistair McFadyen.[4] Basically, McFadyen argues that individuality, or personhood, is not something static which we have before we relate with others (as in Western individualism); nor is it simply thrown up in us by social factors over which we have no control (as in collectivism): rather, personhood is 'dialogical' in nature – that is, we only achieve what is meant by 'personhood' *through a process of engaging with others*.

That is, (and here is *his* definition), " 'I' am a centre of consciousness and will, who achieves individual person-hood by a sedimenting process of interactions with others". It is not that we are fully persons from day one, but that we only *become* persons as we relate to others. God has created us as 'social beings' (McFadyen argues) not merely in the sense that he has made us with the *capacity* for social relations, but that we only *become* true human persons *through* social relations. There are two dimensions to this.

We may say that creation in God's image has a *vertical* component, according to which our personhood is defined by *God's* addressing us and calling us *into communion with him* – a communion like the one that exists between Father, Son and Spirit. This inevitably means that an individual human being will only achieve true personhood when she or he lives in total openness to God and can respond with love. Indeed, when we call Christ 'the image of God', part of our meaning is precisely that in him we see true human personhood, because he lives in perfect communion with the Father through the Spirit. To be made in God's image, there-fore, means that we are created to live in openness and gratitude to the triune, social God who gives each of us our life and addresses each of us as a partner in his world.

The theological core of creation in God's image is that we are created as social beings after the pattern of the trinitarian, social God.

However, creation in God's image also has a *hori-zontal* dimension. It is not an accident that when God said, 'Let us make man in our image', scripture goes on to say that 'in the image of God he created man; *male* and *female* he created them'. Nor is it an accident that when we read the second account of creation in Genesis 2, having made Adam and placed him among the beasts, God still maintained that it was not good for him to be alone and duly created Eve to be his partner. Until this happens, Adam is not truly 'Man' at all. Adam and Eve only become true persons (reflecting God's image) as each relates in openness to the other; as they explore their sameness and distinctness; as each engages the other, mentally, physically, spiritually and emotionally. Adam only becomes 'man' in relation to this other, the 'woman'. They both become true human persons in their communion together (and with God). This is what it means to be 'in God's image'.

I would not wish to suggest that this implies true personhood is only found in marriage. Authentic marriage is a wonderful experience of personhood, but Jesus was the image of God without being married, as was Paul, whom many Protestants would regard as the Lord's chief apostle. But both expressed the image of God in their deep commitment to God and to people.

In short, I think the theological core of creation in God's image is that we are created as social beings after the pattern of the trinitarian, social God. We only become genuinely human persons through the dynamic of relating, loving, confiding in, questioning and being questioned by the other: that is, by God and by our neighbour. Or, in the language of the recent BCC commission on trinity: 'To be a *person* [my italics] ... is to be what one gives to and receives freely from the other persons with whom one is in relationship'.[5] We could playfully offer an alternative to Descartes' fundamental assertion: not 'I think, therefore I am', but 'I relate, therefore I am'.

So, if you fertilised a human ovum and left it totally

isolated in a clever laboratory on a desert island, twenty-one years later you may have something that looked like a human, but 'laboratory Jane' wouldn't have any of that quality that we call personhood – and whether at that stage she could develop any, I am not sure. For those of us who grow up in more normal conditions, we begin to acquire personhood from birth (perhaps even before birth), first in relation to mother and father, and later in relation to siblings, and wider family and social groups.

4. The essence of the fall and its consequences

The nature of the first sin is significant, and generic, to us all. The man and the woman grasp at wisdom ('the knowledge of good and evil') in order to become like God (Gen 3:5). What is wrong is that they seek to achieve such wisdom not in openness and loving communion with God but, rather, in rugged independence from him and against his expressed will. In a sense, Augustine was right: the essence of the sin (of *all* our sin) lies in this self-love, this centering of my personhood, not in the relationships for which I was made, and into which I was called, but in my own centre of consciousness and desires.

The man and the woman wanted the wisdom to become 'independent', and that, alas, was exactly what God decreed as their *fate*. Ironically, their new-found wisdom exposes them as 'naked'. Their 'independence' experienced from the inside is simply 'alienation'. Their joyful and open relationship with God and with each other ceases, shrivels and sours. They hide from God, from each other and from themselves. God's image is not totally lost, however: Adam and Eve are still addressed by God in love, and they still relate together and (to a degree) draw their personality from each other. But there is real separation: Adam's first words before the God he has disobeyed are to throw blame on Eve. There is a sense that from now on they have partly closed themselves off from each other.

If you think of it, most of the obvious sins of the world can be described as a result of this alienation. They stem from my refusal to accept that you belong to me and I belong to you. I would not try to belittle or slander you; I would not ignore you or bar you from the truth I know by lies; I would not be jealous of you; I would not try to manipulate you; *if* I were able fully and authentically to recognise that God has made me in such a way that I belong to you and you to me - and that we can each only reach our full personhood when we honour, love and relate to each other. It is only when I close my heart to you, when I consider my humanity complete without you (and yours to be unimportant to me) and when I push you out of the circle of my life and concerns, that I am liable to belittle, ignore, envy and manipulate.

The story of the fall is ultimately the story of the universal closure of the human heart (albeit in varying degrees). Nevertheless, contrary to some strands of Protestant tradition, the Bible does not teach that humankind entirely lost the image of God at the fall. Genesis 9:6 – clearly envisaging post-fall possibilities – proscribes murder precisely on the grounds that humans are made in God's image (see also 1 Cor 11:7; James 3:9). That image may have become severely weakened and distorted in us, but the implicit teaching of Genesis 1–2 on personhood remains relevant.

Conclusions

We have only begun to open up the discussion. Even if we confined ourselves to the 'biblical' view of personhood, we would obviously need to give attention to the rest of the Old Testament: Genesis 1–3 is clearly only a beginning. As it happens, most agree that those chapters of Genesis are 'programmatic' in the sense that they address the central questions of what the Old Testament has to say about human personhood. From that perspective, what follows in the Old Testament, in all its wonderful detail and nuance, may largely be regarded as 'commentary'.

However, we learn *crucially* about personhood in the light of our knowledge of the life, ministry and death of Jesus. As the one who uniquely lived out the calling to the authentic personhood implied in Genesis 1:26–27, Jesus is hailed as the very image of God (2 Cor 4:4; Col 1:15). You will probably have guessed that my emphasis on the word 'crucially' involves a measure of punning, for it is at the *cross* that we learn the true nature of personhood as radical self-giving love both to God and to our fellow human beings – a love that fully reconciles the alienated.

Looking back on Christ's example, the New Testament writers would recognise that a society of heroic self-sufficient individualists would epitomise not utopia, but the fall. By contrast, Paul (for example) understands salvation and eschatology as the *reversal* of the alienations introduced by Adam. He thus presents a quite different vision of personhood from the individualism of the West. This is arguably presented at its clearest and at greatest length in Ephesians.[6]

According to the programmatic statement in

Ephesians 1:9–10, God's ultimate will for the end of the ages (a plan Paul says has already been launched in Jesus) is to bring the whole cosmos back into full harmony by uniting it in and under Christ. Chapter 2 of Ephesians celebrates how Christ has begun this in the church. 2.11–13 reminds the readers that they were formerly alienated both from God's people Israel, and from God himself. But, according to 2:14–18, Christ has brought peace where there was hostility. He has done this by breaking down the dividing wall between Gentile and Jew, and creating in himself *one new humanity*, which he also fully reconciled to God at the cross. The result is that Jews and Gentiles, who are united to Christ, together now form the heavenly temple, and the place of God's indwelling presence through the Spirit (2:19–23). Insofar as the church *lives* as one united body, it is then a manifest witness, to all the powers that be, of God's radiant world-reconciling wisdom expressed in Christ (Eph 3:6, 8–12).

It is not surprising, then, that Ephesians 4–6 consists of an urgent and extended call to live out – now! – that unity and cosmic eschatological harmony into which the church has been called (so 4:1–6). Paul explains that Christ has given the church its leaders to guide and control the growth of the body towards the eschatological unity (4:7–16; alas, it was certainly not always his experience that leaders worked in that direction!). Paul presupposes that if the new creation will be one of cosmic harmony, then (a) it *will* manifest a corresponding type of personhood, and (b) that the latter should *already* mark the one in Christ. In Ephesians 4:22–24, this is spelt out as the 'putting off' of the old humanity, and the 'putting on' of the new. The old is characterised by 'alienation'; the new by 'unity', expressed in terms of *corporate* growth towards Christ. In keeping with this, the sins Paul especially warns against, are those that divide the community, and the qualities he commends are those that draw it together. An illuminating instance is the very first concrete case he addresses. In 4:25 he tells the churches to put away falsehood, and that everyone should 'speak the truth with his neighbour'. He then explains the reason for this advice: 'for we are members one of another'. Lies are the devices of estranged parties, to keep the other at a comfortable distance from the true self and its knowledge. By contrast, the believer belongs so radically *to* and *for* his brothers and sisters that she cannot fob them off lightly with falsehoods. If they are other limbs with her of the one body, then to lie to them would suggest the foolishness of a hand trying to isolate itself from the arm, chest and head, to which it belongs. It is a step back into the alienation of the humanity of the fall.

Therefore, while the old humanity was characterised by alienation, the new humanity is characterised by unity expressed in terms of corporate growth (as the people of God) towards Christ. In keeping with this, the sins we should watch out for are those that divide the community, and the qualities to encourage are those that draw it together. I suggest that the corporate and united nature of the new humanity should challenge our dominating cultural views of the nature of human 'being'. Individualism is the mark of the old humanity from which we are being saved. We are called instead towards an interrelational understanding of personhood – a kind of personhood which is fashioned in the image of the Trinity and which we see incarnated in Christ.

Endnotes

1   I should perhaps point out that our concept of 'individualism' was *not* an ancient view. In Graeco–Roman and Jewish cultures, there was indeed an understanding of *individuality*, but 'personhood' was understood in the honour/shame matrix of a *society*. Your persona was defined not as your private 'self' but, primarily, as your public 'face'. Questions were naturally asked about the relationship of that 'face' to your 'private' self, but it was the former that counted.

2   For answers to this kind of thinking, see N H Gregersen, W B Drees and U Görman (eds), *The Human Person in Science and Theology*, T&T Clark, 2000.

3   Importantly, 'Mad Max' is only 'mad', totally individualist and largely isolationist, because his previously *relational* personhood was destroyed in the murder, by bikers, of his wife and child.

4   Alistair McFadyen, *The Call to Personhood: A Christian Theory of the Individual in Social Relationships*, Cambridge University Press, 1990.

5   British Council of Churches, *The Forgotten Trinity*, vol 1, 1989, p22.

6   M Turner, '*Mission and Meaninglessness in Terms of "Unity" in Ephesians*', in eds. A Billington, T Lane and M Turner, *Mission and Meaning: Essays Presented to Peter Cotterell*, Paternoster Press, 1995, 138-66.

Chapter 4

The challenge of personhood: '...Therefore I am'

Antony Billington

Who am I?

If the question sounds somewhat clichéd, it is worth bearing in mind that it has kept a lot of people busy over the centuries. And it is worth asking again, because the issues surrounding 'identity' and 'personhood' (to use two shorthand ways of referring to this debate) seem constantly to be up for grabs. It should come as no surprise that Christians have some distinctive things to say about what it means to be a human being. However, the importance of listening to what others say on the subject should be equally clear, and this is what we are attempting to do here.

We begin with one person who offered an answer of sorts.

Scene 1

A study, somewhere in Europe, circa 1637. A coal stove casts its flickering light across an otherwise dark room, revealing books and rolled-up manuscripts piled high in every available space. At the desk sits French philosopher and mathematician René Descartes, quill in hand, scribbling away, pausing only now and then to stroke his chin thoughtfully before starting to write again...

René Descartes was on to something big: a basis for certainty on which to build knowledge, all knowledge. And he would be content with nothing less than constructing this new building from the foundations up. He would begin the task by setting himself to doubt everything(!) until he discovered the one thing that could not be doubted, and that would be the foundation stone for his building. Where could such a crucial structural block be found?

Descartes didn't have too great a start. For some time, he concluded that nothing could be certain. *I can be deceived by my senses*, he thought. *I see the sun 'rising' and 'setting', but the earth might be moving. I can be deceived because I might be dreaming, or seeing things in that coal fire over there (especially after a long stint at the desk). Or*, he went on, *perhaps an evil demon is intent on deceiving me.*

And then it struck him. The only thing he could not doubt was that he was thinking something. Even if he was thinking that he was seeing things, or thinking that he was dreaming, or thinking that he was being tricked, he was still at least thinking! And so came about one of the all-time clever-sounding maxims to slip into conversation at dinner parties – 'I think, therefore I am' (or *cogito ergo sum* in Latin, for those who want to sound really informed!):

> I noticed that while I was trying to think everything false, it must needs be that I, who was thinking this, was something. And observing that this truth, I think, therefore I am [*cogito ergo sum*] was so solid and secure that the most extravagant suppositions of the skeptics could not overthrow it, I judged that I need

not scruple to accept it as the first principle of
philosophy that I was seeking.

(Descartes, *Le Discours de la Méthode*)

In other words, even if I am thinking that I don't exist,
the fact that I am thinking that I don't exist proves that
I must exist! (It is not known for certain whether people
enjoyed Descartes' scintillating conversation down at
the local tavern.)

Descartes not only managed to prove his own existence (to his own satisfaction, at least), he also suggested
something of the nature of that existence. In particular,
he emphasised the *rational* nature of human beings: I am
a subject who thinks. Indeed, reason was to be the
guiding principle of the period of Western history that
followed Descartes, with its view of objective knowledge
and its confidence in science to supply truth about the
world. Alongside this was the notion that the self is
autonomous: not only am I a rational self, I am an *individual* self. In short, the foundation stone on which
knowledge would be built was the thinking, independent self.

Scene 2

*A university anywhere in the Western world, the present day.
We are having to negotiate hordes of eager students as we
proceed down long corridors, in and out of faculty offices and
lecture rooms, through vast libraries with shelf upon shelf of
books and specialist periodicals covering every topic we could
ever care to think of...*

Many disciplines in the 'academic marketplace' tackle

head-on the various theories of what it means to be a person.

After Descartes, philosophy continued to reflect on facets of *human existence and nature*. In 1974, Leslie Stevenson outlined the main views of humanity in Western thinking, taking in Plato, Christianity, Karl Marx, Sigmund Freud, Jean-Paul Sartre, B F Skinner and Konrad Lorenz along the way.[1] The works of these thinkers don't provide the lightest of bedtime reading, but they do offer distinctive perspectives on what constitutes personhood, many of which are around today in various forms.

As far as Marx (1818–83) was concerned, men and women were animals conditioned by society, particularly by economic factors, and locked in class struggle. Not so, according to Sartre (1905–80), who once offered a deliberate pun on Descartes' formula: *opto ergo sum* – 'I choose, therefore I am'. What counts, according to Sartre, is the making of choices. Our ability to choose makes us human, and there is no ultimate meaning to human existence apart from individual commitment to a particular course of action through which we create our own meaning. According to Lorenz (1903–89), however, humans are an evolved animal species, motivated by innate aggression which is normally channelled towards the production of social structures and individual behaviour patterns.

A range of approaches have grown up under the banner of psychology, each seeing the human person in different ways.

In our tour of the university, we now move from the department of philosophy to the department of psychology, where we learn about the science of the *human mind and behaviour*. Freud (1856–1939) and Skinner (1904–90) are notable names here. A range of approaches have grown up under the banner of psychology, each seeing the human person in different ways: some focus on how behaviour is learnt and reinforced; others on emotional issues, mental processes and reasoning; still others look at societal influences, or the physiological aspects of human beings, including genetics and brain chemistry. The related discipline of cognitive science discusses evolutionary biology, consciousness, reason and artificial intelligence. How far can we be thought of as animals with no freedom or moral agency? Is the brain an 'emotional computer' in which certain 'programmes' are installed via genes and culture?

In the area of medical ethics, for instance, debates on genetic research and cloning have a vested interest in understanding what 'persons' are and how they should be treated.

If psychology studies human mind and behaviour, the disciplines of sociology and anthropology look at *human society and culture*, each (you won't be surprised to hear) with its separate branches of theory on the best way of going about this. Some studies point to the importance of 'space'– not the vast, 'final frontier' stuff out there, but the space all around us, where we work and live. Even something as relatively familiar as the physical surroundings of our home can have a powerful influence on how behaviour is organised within a family. The shape of a house expresses implicit beliefs about social order – who does what and where, where work takes place, where sleeping and lovemaking occur, where food is prepared and eaten – and this will be different in different cultures. No less important than this 'spatial' element is the 'temporal' element – time. Our lives had a 'beginning' and will have an 'end', and in between, they are ordered by a pattern of day and night, season after season, birthdays and anniversaries. Once again, different cultures express the significance of this sequence and these events in different ways.

In many of these areas of study, the *human body* as a source of identity is crucial. Our bodies are the means by which we use tools to accomplish tasks and through which we socialise. The body too has its own 'space', which can be modified and redeveloped like any other. Because our bodies have needs (food, clothing, shelter) they can be thought of as 'consumer' bodies. We may not always think this way, but you can be sure that someone in charge of the local shopping centre does!

In case we are tempted to think that all this is academic irrelevance, we should realise the profound practical implications such thinking can have. In the area of medical ethics, for instance, debates on genetic research and cloning have a vested interest in understanding what 'persons' are and how they should be treated. This will only become more complicated as human genes are patented and human life becomes a commercial commodity. Suddenly, the question 'Who am I?' takes on a certain urgency.

Scene 3

A high street newsagent. Racks of colourful, glossy magazines are displayed to catch the eye wherever we look. We're quite glad to be out of the university – all that stuff on 'identity' and 'personhood' was starting to hurt the brain! But it only takes a moment's reflection to realise that we haven't escaped. We are surrounded by dozens of 'voices' all offering different views on what it means to be a person in today's world – only this time they are more subtle...

While the more academic disciplines address the topic of personhood explicitly, it is more difficult, but possibly more rewarding, to consider the many areas of contemporary culture which are also expressing a view on human identity, only *implicitly*. Magazines provide one source of reflection. Try it when you're next in a large newsagent. What do the titles, cover stories, features, pictures and advertisements say about how contemporary men, women and young people understand themselves?

Some years back, the Social Affairs Unit offered an assessment of women's magazines under the title *The British Woman Today*.[2] They concluded that although some magazines hold to 'traditional' values, in the vast majority of cases 'magazine woman' has no children, sees relationships as purely about sex, views life as principally about indulging herself, lives in a value-free world, treats tragedies and freaks as entertainment, and finds reality rather awkward. Not particularly flattering! The Social Affairs Unit has yet to offer their view of men's magazines, but it's not clear that the male of the species would fare any better in their assessment.

Apart from regular magazines aimed generally at men and women, there are other, more specialised publications which appeal to certain sub-groups.

I holiday, therefore I am

They're the first things to go into my diary. My yearly calendar is punctuated by blocks marked out two or three times at regular intervals. A week here. Two weeks there. Somewhere abroad. Somewhere hot. Somewhere to ski. Maybe somewhere closer to home next year. Then again, maybe not. Although they don't say it outright, I know that my acquaintances think I live for my holidays. But they don't understand that I really do need the break...

I invest, therefore I am

Finance means security, after all. It's only sensible to know your PEPs from your ISAs, from your TESSAs, your fixed rates from your variable rates, your policies, endowments and pensions. It can be quite interesting once you get into it, you know! And I don't do this for my own sake – I've got my kids to think about. You've got to prepare for the future, haven't you?

I exercise, therefore I am

Well, actually, I'd like to exercise a little more than I do. But then, who doesn't? I'm not so stupid as to think I could ever really have that washboard stomach/those sculpted quads/those rounded breasts/that pert back-side, but I'm pretty sure I could come close if I worked on it. I *will* work on it when I've got more time. I might even start next week...

I party, therefore I am

I haven't really got around to reading the magazine but I do listen to the cover CD! It reminds me of when we went to Ibiza last year. It's not quite the same atmosphere in the Blue Lagoon club on Saturday nights, but we try not to admit it to each other, and we still have a laugh after all...

I cruise, therefore I am

I'm talking cars here – souped-up engines, big exhausts, fat tyres, trims, stripes, shiny bonnets, preferably with half-naked women stretched out over them. I'm also talking hi-fi systems with lots of buttons, lights and tweakers, woofers and speakers, preferably with half-naked women stretched out over them...

The list could go on, and you can add your own. Magazines dealing with shopping, fashion, gardening, science, current affairs, TV, gossip, music, electronic equipment, technology, computers, the Web, pets, football, golf, mountain bikes, motorbikes, caravans, boats, art and craft, woodwork, model railways, treasure hunting, family trees and much more, offer windows on to some of the factors that make up the human identity in contemporary society. 'Who am I?' The answers are out there.

Scene 4

The local multiplex, one of those multi-screen cinemas increasingly found attached to a large shopping centre, which offers simulated worlds on top of simulated worlds. And you don't even have to leave the building! We buy some toiletries from an English medieval soaphouse, some clothes from an American gas station, get something to eat in a Mediterranean port, before wondering whether to go to the Saharan Desert with Kristin Scott-Thomas or to outer space with Bruce Willis...

One set of magazines we didn't mention in the last scene – although we certainly can't miss them on any news-stand – are those devoted to cinema and DVD. Films provide much of the 'cultural currency' in which discussions about life, death and all things between take place. What do movies say about who we are as humans? In fact, all forms of art and media serve both as a major source of meaning, as well as the means through which we express our dreams and fears, hopes and aspirations. So, if you don't particularly enjoy visiting the cinema, or the examples in this section mean little to you, try the same exercise with art and sculpture, or literature, or architecture, or fashion...

I am reflecting on human existence, nature and destiny

Interestingly, some types (or genres) of film offer explicit reflections on what it means to be human: science fiction, in particular, raises questions as to how crucial our bodies are for understanding what it means to be human. What, if anything, defines a person over against, say, a robot? In Ridley Scott's *Blade Runner* (1982), 'replicants' (artificial humans) strive to establish their identity as persons in their own right. Similar issues are at stake in the more recent *X-Men* (2000), based on the superhero comic of the same title. Cyborgs frequently function as counterparts to humans, marking the boundaries of humanness against technology; but what happens when those boundaries are confused? Science fiction offers reflections on the space we occupy (often compounded with time travel) and explores the importance of memory for human identity (eg *Robocop* [1987]; *Total Recall* [1990]). But though science fiction is sometimes thought to be about the future, it is really our present hopes and fears that are being projected onto the future. It should come as no surprise, then, that science fiction can be both optimistic and pessimistic.

In *The Matrix* (1999), computers rule the world and use the energy produced by humans, suspended embryo-like in incubator tanks, as their power source. The humans' minds roam in a simulated world – the 'Matrix' – an artificial reality, which acts as a mental prison. But humans don't know they are prisoners and so feel no need to escape, happily assuming they exist in the 'ordinary' world. However, there are some renegades who know the truth and are seeking the One who will be able to destroy the Matrix and liberate humans from bondage.

Science fiction thus deals with human destiny, and here Hollywood has certainly tapped into a popular 'apocalyptic' fascination with the end of the world. Whether it's Will Smith attacking aliens in *Independence Day* (1996), Bruce Willis destroying meteors in *Armageddon* (1998) or Arnold Schwarzenegger fighting Satan in *End of Days* (1999), Hollywood's version of the apocalypse tends to put human beings in charge of their own destiny. The threatening apocalyptic scenario can even be avoided by human ingenuity.

A number of Arnold Schwarzenegger's starring roles have been science fiction flicks, most recently *The 6th Day* (2000). The film's title and the name of the main character (Adam) clearly invite us to place its story alongside the creation account in Genesis. Aspects of human identity are also to the fore in his earlier *The Terminator* (1984), and *Terminator 2: Judgement Day* (1991). In the second film, the growing relationship between the boy (John Connor) and the protecting cyborg brings out elements of what it is to be human.

The boy's mother, Sarah, reflects that 'of all the would-be fathers who came and went over the years, this thing, this machine, was the only one who measured up'. The final act of self-sacrifice on the part of the android draws the comment from Sarah that 'if a machine can learn the value of human life, maybe we can too'.

I am negotiating the tension between the domestic and the dramatic

If science fiction offers an obvious opportunity to reflect on the nature of human identity, every movie genre can be explored for what it communicates implicitly about personhood – even films which, on the face of it, seem fairly superficial, like action movies.

Interestingly, although Schwarzenegger's characters are sometimes held to be the epitome of masculinity (albeit caricatured, thankfully!), a number of his films integrate the roles of 'father' with 'action hero' – *Commando* (1985), *Kindergarten Cop* (1990), *The Last Action Hero* (1993). *In True Lies* (1994), he plays a spy whose job is concealed from his bored wife and dysfunctional daughter, who think he's a computer salesman. His wife's excitement comes from a relationship with a used-car salesman who poses as a spy to pick up women. The film plots how his wife and then his daughter are drawn into real spy action, before it reunites them happily at the end.

In fact, with some exceptions (James Bond being a notable example), most action movie heroes are placed ambiguously between the world of family and domesticity, and the world of action and adventure. In *Face/Off* (1997), starring Nicolas Cage and John Travolta, the change of face the characters undergo arguably leads to a kind of redemption for each man. As Sean Archer, Castor Troy cares about the agent's family life, an aspect of life that he himself has neglected. As Castor Troy, Sean Archer tries to make amends for the terrorist's actions, particularly regarding his lack of care for his child, who is brought into his own household at the end. Only as they walk in one another's shoes (literally, wear one another's faces) are the two men able to see aspects of one another's lives that would otherwise be closed to them, and this has domestic pay-offs in each case. Likewise with Nicolas Cage's character, Stanley Goodspeed, in *The Rock* (1996). He has a lab job (when he's not forced into becoming a field agent), and drives a beige Volvo (when he's not engaged in a high-speed chase in a yellow Ferrari), and enjoys life with his pregnant fiancée (when he's not saving her from becoming a victim of the nerve gas threat on San Francisco).

The same tension is brought to the fore in *The Long Kiss Goodnight* (1996) in Geena Davies' character as Samantha Caine (a schoolteacher, living with a man and her eight-year-old daughter) and Charly Baltimore (an assassin for the government). Much of the film revolves around the struggle between the homemaker and the assassin, the realm of the domestic and the realm of the action, moving towards some sort of reconciliation. Similar themes are found in the *Lethal Weapon* films (1987 onwards). Mel Gibson's character, Martin Riggs, begins the series as a suicidal and jaded cop, suffering emotional damage after the death of his wife. But by *Lethal Weapon IV* (1998), he's contemplating growing old and getting married, and even becomes a father at the end of the movie!

I am portraying a broken condition which needs mending

Comedy provides a different way of reflecting on humanity. Much was made of Elizabeth Hurley's turn as the devil in *Bedazzled* (2000), but the film arguably has more to say about the predicament of human person-hood than it does about the work of Satan. In that sense, it is more helpful to compare it with some of Harold Ramis' other films, such as *Groundhog Day* (1993), about a news reporter wrestling with his duality, and *Multiplicity* (1996), about a construction worker wrestling with his duality, and *Analyze This* (1999), about a mobster (yes, you've guessed it) wrestling with his duality.

The well-received *American Beauty* (1999) holds up a mirror in which men and women may see themselves reflected. The voiceover of the main character tells us at the start that within a year he'll be dead and then goes on: 'But in a way I'm dead already.' The film depicts not only his mid-life crisis (shown most obviously by his crush on his teenage daughter's girlfriend) but also portrays human weakness; the deep needs of a broken world disconnected from family, friends and self; and the need for meaningful relationships. But it is as much about compassion as it is about alienation, and tries to point towards 'transcendence', to look beyond conven-tional beauty to discover *real* beauty in the not-so-obvious places (among other things, in the way that Ricky's video of the blowing bag calls us to look beyond the entrapments of everyday life).

The Truman Show (1998), starring Jim Carrey, is of a piece with a fair bit of recent interest in the notion of human beings as media animals. The success of Channel

4's *Big Brother* indicates something of our fascination with watching other human beings. We are given the opportunity, for a limited period at least, to be that scary, George Orwellian thing – 'Big Brother'. A number of reviewers suggested Truman should be seen as a 'true man' – a truly authentic human being, seeking the truth about the world, and ultimately the truth about himself. Our media culture may surround us with simulations that masquerade as something authentic. However, so far as *The Truman Show* is concerned, if we want to be free and authentic human beings, we have to be willing to live in the world as it is.

The success of Channel 4's *Big Brother* indicates something of our fascination with watching other human beings.

What *The Truman Show* doesn't know is that God doesn't take us out of the real world... He is with us, in it.

Scene 5

The Last Day, at some undisclosed time in the future. We are witnessing nothing less than the end of the old creation and the beginning of the new.

Our world-view cannot be based on contemporary culture, for even at its best it is a poor reflection of God's truth. However much we can learn about human identity from the contemporary world, Christians will want to engage with it from the perspective of a distinctive Christian world-view founded on scripture. There are two significant ways of achieving this: one way is to consider the *story* the Bible tells; the other is to consider the *literature* the Bible contains. Only then will we be able to appreciate fully the perspective the Bible brings on this question of our human identity.

The story the Bible tells

Christians have looked to the biblical account of creation for their understanding of what it means to be human and created in the image of God. The opening chapters of Genesis consider the place of humans in relationship to the world (which we are called to take care of on God's behalf) and each other (there is an undeniable social dimension to human nature, not least in the sexual differentiation of Adam and Eve). Overarching all this is our capacity to relate to God – or not, as the case turns out. For Genesis goes on to show how human sin has tragic effects on our relationship with the world, with each other and with God. Fortunately, the biblical story goes on to tell of God becoming flesh and living among us (John 1:14). God himself is 'embodied' in what Christians call 'the incarnation' – not as an end in itself, but because the only way we can be rescued from sin and restored to full humanity is through the restoration achieved by Jesus' death on the cross on our behalf.

And the story doesn't end there, for while we belong to the church of Christ, a people in whom God's Spirit lives, we look forward to Jesus' return, the remaking of the universe, and new bodies. Until then, we remain 'on the way' to becoming fully human, true images of God, with our identity finally complete at the end of the story.

The literature the Bible contains

One of the most helpful ways of gathering together what

the Bible says on a particular issue is to do so on the basis of its different literary genres (eg law, narrative, wisdom) and asking how each contributes to the big picture. Such an approach allows us to take account of the creation of human beings in the image of God; to see the dynamics of human relationship in the narratives that follow (in Jacob's family, or the stories of Samson and David); and to appreciate how God works on behalf of his people, sometimes openly (in Exodus) and sometimes not so openly (in the account of Joseph or the book of Ruth). The various Old Testament laws make quite clear the value of the individual person (men, women, children, workers) in fellowship with others, as well as the human connection to land and social order. The psalms depict something of the relationship of the individual and the community with God, giving rise to shouts of praise and thanksgiving, as well as cries of pain and repentance. The Song of Songs offers a poetic celebration of human sexuality. Other parts of the wisdom literature further reflect on facets of experience in the real world, where the very practical matters of how I do my job, speak about others, bring up my children, conduct my finances, and treat my spouse are founded on my 'fear of the Lord' (Prov 1:7).

And so we could go on, through the prophets, the Gospels and the epistles, right through to the book of Revelation and the final vision of humanity communing with Almighty God and the Lamb. Each biblical genre offers a distinctive slant on what it is to be human, and each needs the others to give an undistorted picture of that humanity.

The perspective the Bible brings

We need, therefore, to look at the various literary genres in scripture within the context of the biblical story, stretching from creation to the new creation. Only then will we able to address the needs and aspirations of contemporary culture without assimilating them into a tamed biblical text.

Our brief tour through contemporary disciplines and select aspects of popular culture should be enough to show the many strands that make up the notion of human identity. But the Bible is no less complex and rich in the threads it weaves. It places great importance on the *individual* but does not reduce people to Descartes' thinking, autonomous self. It stresses the importance of relationship which, as Christian theologians have not been slow to point out, is grounded in God's own trinitarian nature – Father, Son and Holy Spirit – where true personhood is to be found. Dignity is ascribed to human beings; whatever we may believe about the mechanics of creation, the Bible does not reduce us to evolved animals or vast assemblies of nerve cells. Economic struggle and behavioural environment are given their due, but humans are not locked into those criteria or identified solely by them. Wherever the body may be devalued, the Bible reminds us that Christianity centres on the notion of *embodied* existence in Christ's incarnation.

Contemporary culture may offer views on the future, not least in apocalyptic films (as we have seen). But, as the Christian interacts with such films, he or she will do so on the presuppositions of the biblical view of hope, where God is ultimately in charge of human destiny. So we can expect a biblical standpoint on personhood at some time to connect with contemporary world-views and sometimes to challenge them. As we engage with such perspectives, we must continually seek to do so on the basis of a Christian world-view shaped by scripture, which moulds the way we view God, the world and ourselves as his image-bearers.

Endnotes

1   Leslie Stevenson, *Seven Theories of Human Nature*, Oxford University Press, 1974.

2   Digby Anderson and Michael Mosbacher (eds), *The British Woman Today: A Qualitative Survey of the Images in Women's Magazines*, The Social Affairs Unit, 1997.

Chapter 5

The challenge of consumerism: We're all shopaholics now

Derek Tidball

Saturday afternoons used to be a bore. Our family never indulged in the pleasure of a first division football match – that would have been 'worldly'. For us, Saturday afternoon meant the weekly shop. Bundled into the car, we would make our way to the nearby small market town, where we would traipse around in what felt like a never-ending tedious ritual of popping in and out of the multitude of tiny high street stores. The drudgery was only relieved by the purchase of a delicious chocolate bar from the half dozen or so to choose from in Woolworths. The men (or boys), of course, protested more than the women: for them, at least, shopping was a chore.

How things have changed. Shopping, which used to be arch-enemy number one, has become leisure-choice number one. For the vast majority, it has been transformed into a pleasure. The tiny high street stores have given way to the enticing Aladdin's cave of the shopping mall, often removed from the high street, where warmth and colour seductively beckon the consumer inside. The mall self-consciously boasts 'the food court' and the multiplex cinema which serve to underline the message that the boundary between buying and leisure is entirely artificial. It has become so pleasurable, in fact, that it is seen as a means of healing: we speak of it as 'retail therapy'.

Equally, shopping has become an act full of religious significance. The architecture of the shopping mall often imitates the older architecture of the village church, complete with clock and steeple, revealing its true iden-

Shopping has become an act full of religious significance.

tity. The shopping mall is the temple where the consumers practise their religious rituals (until the Internet takes over, if it ever does) and bow down before the idols of fashion displayed in the various shrines of the market economy.

What has happened to bring about this transformation? What effect does it have in shaping our thinking? How should Christians respond?

By the end of the twentieth century, consumerism had become an extremely potent cultural force. The advanced techniques of mass-production, foreshadowed by Henry Ford in the car industry, combined with the techniques of creative marketing and the use of radio and television to turn us all into consumers.[1] Full employment and surplus cash meant that we had the resources to become consumers. Consuming was no longer what we did, it was what we had *become*. Hence the frequently quoted adage *Tesco ergo sum*[2] (I shop, therefore I am) has replaced the older Enlightenment understanding of what forms our identity summed up in Descartes' phrase *Cogito ergo sum* (I think, therefore I am).

From earliest times people have engaged in some form of exchange of goods, so commercial activity is nothing new: it was inherent in the logic of the modern industrialised and capitalist world. But, as Craig Bartholomew points out, we need to distinguish between *commerce* and *consumerism*.[3] Consumerism is commerce taken to its illogical conclusion, for it makes us purchase things we do not need. It is commerce cheapened, for it leads us to know 'the price of everything and the value of nothing'. It is commerce run riot, for we become its slave rather than it submitting to us as masters.[4]

The Bible and material possessions

The distinction between commerce and consumerism is helpful, not least in helping us to understand what the Bible teaches about material possessions, and to relate it to the world in which we live.[5] The Bible often seems to celebrate material prosperity in a way that causes many of us to blush (unless we have bought into the distorted and unwarranted 'gospel of prosperity'), since we have heard materialism denounced so often from the pulpit as a heinous sin. Yet the Lord is the one who boasts that 'every animal of the forest is mine, and the cattle on a thousand hills' (Ps 50:10). His glory is served by 'the wealth of the nations' being brought as gifts to the restored Jerusalem (Isa 60, especially verse 11). How does this fit?

Four elements of the Bible's teaching in this area may help:

- We need to see all we have as a gift from God rather than as something we possess as of right. Again and again, the people of Israel were taught that the land of which they had taken possession was not theirs, but a gift of God, a land inherited because of his promise rather than because they had a right to it (eg Deut 8:10–18). In the New Testament, Paul echoes the same principle in asking the arrogant Corinthians what it is they have that they did not receive as a gift (1 Cor 4:7).

- We need to avoid idolatry at all times – the idolatry of absolutising and worshipping things made by human hands. To do so is logically absurd (since we made them) and spiritually destructive (Isa 46:5–10; Jer 10:1–16).

- Even in the midst of celebrating God's goodness to us, we need to remember the poor. Apart from the wider teaching about care for the poor in the Bible, the book of Nehemiah brings the issue into sharp focus when God's repentant people are told not to mourn and weep, but to 'go and enjoy choice food and sweet drinks, and send some to those who have nothing prepared' (Neh 8:10). It is right to celebrate God's bountiful provision, which is his creation intention for all people, but not to do so in such a way that it becomes an exercise in social irresponsibility and self-indulgence.

- We need to receive everything with deliberate and spoken thanksgiving to God (1 Tim 4:4–5). The exercise of this spiritual discipline will save us from arrogance, deliver us from a 'rights' mentality and make us a grateful, as opposed to a grasping, people. We need to verbalise our thanks to God, perhaps saying grace before a meal, in some other act of prayer, or by consciously reminding each other of God's blessing on us. If we only express our thankfulness silently, we are likely soon to take its expression for granted and then cease to be thankful altogether.

Consumerism and contemporary society

Our concern here is more with a Christian's attitude to consumerism than a Christian's attitude to material possessions. Consumerism affects much more than our shopping habits: it affects the way we live life on a much broader canvas than that. The consumer mentality has become deeply ingrained as a way of seeing the world, and now touches almost every aspect of our social and our working lives.

Consumerism says that everything can be 'commodified'

In a consumerist society we produce, market, sell and buy 'commodities'. Commodities are simply things that we trade. When we used the word in the past, we were referring to things like washing machines, cars, fridges and televisions. They were tangible goods which someone had manufactured and which were then sold on to us through a retail outlet of some sort. But now *everything* is seen as a commodity: health, education, services, law and order, culture, even religion has become 'commodified'.

The impact of the consumer mentality has been extremely visible in the health service. Doctors have become fundholders, and beds in hospitals have to be 'purchased'. When one health authority has sold its stock of particular operations, negotiations must be entered into with others to see if they can supply them. The culture is one of managerial contracts rather than the covenanted service that used to characterise doctors and hospitals. Productive efficiency is measured not only so that the costs can be calculated exactly, but so that the customers can see the relative value of a particular health authority by where they are in the league tables.

It is the same across the board. Take literary culture as another example: that too has become 'commodified'. The classic novels continue in circulation because they can be abridged and packaged for television. When the series is on, or the film is released, sales of the books go up. They are not commended as elevating to the mind, still less to the spirit, but as a racy story or a scandalous adventure. They are presented not for their own sakes but to ensure that the TV channel wins the ratings war it perpetually wages against its rivals. 'Culture' therefore becomes accessible to all, which may in itself be a good thing. But in the process it has changed and become a matter of consumer choice and purchasable just like a kettle or a mobile phone.

The church is just as vulnerable to the forces of consumerism as anyone else. But more of that later.

Consumerism says that everything must be marketed

If everything is capable of being reduced to a commodity, we can see then that the logic is that it must be marketed. Stiff competition means than advertising becomes more and more frenetic, and reaches into areas which hitherto have been advertising-free zones. No longer does electricity just arrive in our house from the one public supplier – we are bombarded by gas companies who want to sell us cheaper electricity than the electricity industry can itself. The phone company uses the phone more than the customers do to convince you that you can't do without that unique special offer available only to its three million most favoured customers. Universities tout for business by advertising for students in local bus stations because they need to widen access to higher education and attract those who previously would never have thought of studying for a degree. Numbers need to be kept up so that government grants can be obtained and good positions secured in the league tables *vis à vis* their competitors.

We have already mentioned the marketing of literary culture, but the connection between culture and commerce is even more evident at the popular end of the market. There the alliance between the empires of Disney and McDonald's is potent. No film stands on its own. No cartoon or children's programme takes place in isolation. No Disney animation is just for entertainment. It's all about business – the business of getting people to watch the movie at the cinema and buy the toys, the clothes, the books, the watches, the stationery, the videos, the DVDs, the umbrellas, the trinkets and the hamburgers which continue to proclaim its message. They all reinforce each other: the sale of one item leads to the sale of a range of items.

It's the same with the church. From Coca-cola to cars to clergy, they all have to be marketed. If we have not yet reached the point, unlike leaders in politics, where bishops are elected primarily for their media skills and telegenic personalities, we are not far off. Everything must be marketed.

The values and effects of consumerism

Consumerism is not a neutral fact of contemporary life. It is one which powerfully configures our mindset. It carries within it values that are all the more dangerous because we take them for granted. Let's select five to think about.

1 Consumerism is self-centred

When I go to the supermarket, 'I' am a powerful person for 'I' am a consumer. That puts me at the centre of every transaction. If I don't find the brand name of something I want on the shelves, in the size I want, at the price I want, I'll shop somewhere else that can supply me more to my satisfaction. If I find what I want, in the right quantity and at the right price, I will buy it. It is not quite right to say that customer choice dictates all, because there are other, more hidden forces at work (the forces of marketing and fashion). We are not quite the free human beings we like to think we are. Even so, we are powerful. Ask the publisher Dorling Kindersley! When customers refused to buy the quantities of *Stars Wars* books they had produced, they made huge losses and had to sell the company.[6] Ask the great supermarket chains why they're so concerned about 'customer services' and reduced check-out queues. It's because the customer is 'prince', if not 'king', in a consumer society. And the customer measures everything by himself – *his* likes, wants, desires, needs, timetable and taste (or 'hers', as the gender may be).

> In the beginning of this narrative is the self-made, self sufficient human being. At the end of this narrative is the big house, the big car and the expensive clothes. in the middle is the struggle for success, the greed, the getting, the spending in a world where there is no such thing as a free lunch. Most of us have made this so thoroughly 'our story' that we are hardly aware of its influence.
>
> (Susan White, quoted in Craig Bartholomew and Thorsten Moritz [eds], 'Christ and Consumerism', Paternoster, 2000, p2)

2 Consumerism exalts choice

A recent survey discovered that anyone who undertook a serious review of all the options available in mobile phones, to find out which was the very best for them, would take 150 years to complete it – by which time the mobile phone would no longer be of any use.[7] This research only highlights the absurd degree of diversity with which we are confronted. We can easily be made punch-drunk with choice. Think how many varieties of breakfast cereal call out to us from the supermarket shelves.

Some handle the diversity by refusing to make a choice at all. I did when it came to mobile phones: I didn't have the time or the energy to choose. I refused to have one, until my wife gave me one as a birthday present! Many more people, however, see choice as a right we all have as individuals in an increasingly individualised society. We assume that we ought to be able to choose to get just exactly what we want and when we want it. It is the outworking of a long process of political democracy and freedom, as well as the advance of technology, which makes an ever-increasing variety of products a viable option.[8]

Long ago (when the pluralism of modernity of which he and others were writing looked like the scribblings of a kindergarten child compared to the adolescent version of postmodern pluralism we encounter today) Peter Berger pointed out that such choice leads us to a condition of homelessness.[9] We never belong or settle anywhere. We simply migrate from one position to another, one experience to another, one product to another. 'It goes without saying,' Berger wrote, 'that this condition is psychologically hard to bear.' Serious questions are being asked as to whether the rise in the incidence of depression is not related to having too much choice. If we can't choose, we buy (or believe) what's put in front of us. But if we can choose, we become anxious as to whether we have chosen (or believed) rightly or whether we have wasted our money, energy or commitments on the wrong thing.

Choice is, of course, the luxury of the Western world: elsewhere it is very different. While we worry every few months about the best way to update our computer technology, and are confronted by bewildering choice, it is still a fact that the majority of people in the world have still not made a single telephone call! While we puzzle over which of the twenty-three kinds of breakfast cereal to buy, it is still a fact that thousands die of hunger every day.

3 Consumerism becomes addictive

We no longer confine shopping to the necessary chore of obtaining essentials in order to live. Shopping has become something we do regardless of need. Buying has become a compulsive activity: we do it whether we need what we buy or not. The more we do it, the more we want to do it. It is habit-forming and dependency-creating, like a drug that enslaves. We are a nation of shopping junkies, and the advertising industry and the working of our economy conspire to keep our habit fed.

Paul's words to the Corinthians are apt in this situation. Writing about fulfilling sexual desire he first of all quotes their popular slogans and then puts in his own riposte: ' "Everything is permissible for me" – but not everything is beneficial. "Everything is permissible for me" – but I will not be mastered by anything' (1 Cor 6:12). Christians should be free from all controlling forces in their lives except the liberating, controlling force of Christ.

4 Consumerism shapes our values

No longer does our society determine our values and then, as a consequence of what we treasure, shape our consumption accordingly: rather, the reverse is true. We first determine what we can sell and then derive our values from our consumption.[10] Hence designer clothes and the fashion industry determine the right 'image', and image is all. We are not schooled to look beyond image to character. Sex is marketable, so sex must be disconnected from any moral framework to do with the commitment of one man and one woman in lifelong marriage: people must be able to purchase it whenever they choose. The pressure to remove restrictions on pornography is logical in such a society: if it sells, it must be right. And sell we must, 364 days a year,[11] seven days a week and (increasingly) twenty-four hours a day. The deregulation of trading hours betrays our true values. We worship consumerism and no longer value the idea of space created by the shops being closed. We don't want to preserve space for religious worship, family life or wholesome recreation – factors which used to determine our values – because the value that dictates all is the right to shop.

We judge the rightness of something by whether or not it sells rather than by any deeper moral principles. Similarly, we judge the 'value' of entertainment, music, television programmes and films by where they come in the charts or the ratings tables. If it can sell, people must not be denied it, for that would limit their freedom. So, with few exceptions, the freedom to purchase is seen as an inalienable right, just as much as the freedom of speech and freedom of religion for which our forebears fought. The exceptions (like selling glue and alcohol to under eighteen-year-olds) betray something of society's uneasy conscience at the margins, but they are not to be taken too seriously. Politicians have been recklessly travelling down the one-way street of deregulating most things in the moral sphere in recent years, with the result that the state has moved out of all areas of defining value as far as our sexual, family and social lifestyles are concerned, leaving the high priests of consumerism to preach what is right and what is wrong from the pulpit of choice. If ever a pulpit were six foot above contradiction, that one is!

5 Consumerism promises freedom

We have all been fooled. Consumerism has sold us a lie. It tells us that if only we have the latest fashionable clothes, the most up-to-date IT system, that Caribbean cruise, the bigger house, then we shall have freedom; we will be fulfilled; we will shake off the frustrations of life that we currently feel, and fill the aching void inside.[12] Of course, it never happens. The addictive nature of consumerism means than when we have bought the latest thing, there is something else we desperately want. Like the Russian doll, we remove one layer only to find another underneath, and we never get to the end.

Far from delivering freedom, consumerism is an idolatry that enslaves.

The leech has two daughters. 'Give! Give!' they cry.
There are three things that are never satisfied, four
that never say, 'Enough!':
the grave, the barren womb,
land, which is never satisfied with water,
and fire, which never says, 'Enough!'

(Proverbs 30:15–16)

Spiritual consumers

The consumerist mentality has made serious inroads into the way we practise our Christian lives. Three examples will suffice.

1 Consumerism and our relation with God

No one has articulated our changing view of God more accurately or more passionately than David Wells. He writes of the way in which we no longer view God as sovereignly awesome, whose words we must obey: rather, he has been reduced in our minds until he is 'weightless':

> We have turned to a God that we can use rather than a God we must obey; we have turned to a God who will fulfil our needs rather than to a God before whom we must surrender our rights to ourselves. He is a God for us, for our satisfaction – not because we have learned to think of him this way through Christ but because we have learned to think of him this way through the marketplace. In the marketplace, everything is for us, for our pleasure, for our satisfaction, and we have come to assume that it must be so in the church as well. And so we transform the God of mercy into a God who is at our mercy.

> We will not be able to recover the vision and under-
> standing of God's grandeur until we recover an
> understanding of ourselves as creatures who have
> been made to know such grandeur. This must begin
> with the recovery of the idea that as beings made in
> God's image, we are fundamentally moral beings, not
> consumers, that the satisfaction of our psychological
> needs pales in significance when compared with the
> enduring value of doing what is right. Religious
> consumers want to have a spirituality for the same
> reason that they want to drive a stylish and expensive
> auto. Costly obedience is as foreign to them in matters
> spiritual as self-denial is in matters material.
>
> (David Wells, *God in the Wasteland*, InterVarsity Press,
> 1994, pp114,115)

From our faulty view of God, other consumerist attitudes flow to emaciate our Christian lives.

2 Consumerism and our relation to the Bible

Craig Bartholomew points out how foreign it is for any
university department of theology to view the Bible as
God's word.[13] It has been so for a long time, but in its
most recent phase scholars are no longer sure that the
biblical text can be said to have a true meaning, but only
a variety of different interpretations put forward by a
plurality of scholars. The marketplace of ideas that cluster
around the banner of hermeneutics reduces clarity and
certainty, but is positively welcomed by academic institu-
tions. It means you can make the Bible say what you like
and convincingly argue that it says the exact opposite of
what it appears to be saying.

Ordinary Christians (as opposed to academic
scholars!) are just as guilty of doing the same, even if they

do not use the fancy academic apparatus of intellectu-
alism to justify it. We pick and choose the bits of the
Bible that suit us. We read it selectively and interpret it
to our own advantage. We ignore the uncomfortable
parts, or write off those that jar with contemporary
culture. We 'pick and mix' the Bible's message just as we
do sweets in a confectioner's, to make our reading of it
comfortable and ensure that we do not seriously diverge
from the pervading consumer culture.

3 Consumerism and the church

The most obvious sign of consumerism is seen in the
way we 'do' church today. Churches have become shops
which we visit to satisfy our needs, rather than covenant
communities to which we belong no matter what. If the
church is unable to supply our needs – either in terms of
worship style, length of sermon, provision of youth clubs
or whatever – then we shop around until we find one
that does. The thought that what churches believe
about the way they govern their lives, practise the sacra-
ments, or view themselves in relation to the world (all
matters which previous generations held to be the
crucial distinctions between one church and another)
often never crosses our minds.

We pick and choose the limits of our involvement in
church to suit ourselves. At church, just as in the supermarket, we are the customers whom the managers have
to keep happy. We are at the centre of the transaction.
So the issue is not just that we will go to any church that
suits us, just for as long as it suits us, but that we will use
the church rather than belong to it.[14] We view it as something they do for us. We say, 'They should run a Sunday

School for our children', but are not prepared to get involved and teach ourselves. We stand on the sidelines and criticise others for not being involved in sharing the leadership of the church, while justifying our own lack of involvement because of the pressure of other work or family responsibilities. This is why, at least in part, many churches have responded by employing more and more staff, like administrators and youth workers, rather than being able to rely on voluntary help from the members.[15] Too often we are as much consumers in church on Sundays as we are in the shopping arcade on Saturdays.

Space forbids us from developing another aspect of consumerism: that the church is preoccupied with 'marketing' the gospel. Few see any difference between evangelism and marketing, and think purely on a horizontal plane, leaving spiritual dynamics out of the equation altogether.

Consumers or disciples?

As Christians we are called to be disciples, not consumers. We are called to live in a way that stands in profound contradiction to the dominant culture in which we live. We are called to be disciples of Jesus Christ. A disciple is one who, by definition, has a personal attachment to a master which shapes the whole of life and leaves no doubt as to who is in charge.[16] Christ, not we, is at the centre of the transaction. To be his disciple means that:

> We will follow our Master, without regard to personal cost or popularity, just as the earliest disciples did (Mark 1:17,20; 2:14; Luke 5:28).

We will accept his teaching, be it ever so revolutionary, without equivocation. This means not just his teaching on the bits with which we agree, like sexual ethics, but on our relationship to the poor (Luke 14:7–14) or on our style of leadership (Mark 10:42–45) or on not holding grudges (Matt 5:43–48).

We will adopt his companions, even if they would not be our personal choice. If they follow him, however imperfectly, they are one with us (as the original disciples had to learn, Mark 9:38–41).

We will imitate his lifestyle, however countercultural that may prove to be. Perhaps it is at the point of living simply that we need to imitate him most (Matt 8:20).[17] We need to learn afresh that it is in losing our life that we will gain it (Mark 8:34–38). What does it profit us if we possess all our consumerist world has to offer, at the expense of forfeiting a truer, deeper life with God?

As Christians, we should enjoy God's rich creation, and the wonderful things available through human hands as a result, without being seduced by the lie of consumerism. Each generation faces a different challenge as to what it means to be authentic disciples. For our generation, the challenge is to shake ourselves free from the shackles of consumerism.

Endnotes

1   Andrew Walker, *Telling the Story: Gospel, Mission and Culture*, SPCK, 1996, p143; and Craig Bartholomew, 'Christ and consumerism: an introduction', in Craig Bartholomew and Thorsten Moritz (eds), *Christ and Consumerism: Critical Reflections on the Spirit of our Age*, Paternoster, 2000, p5.

2   'Tesco' is not to my knowledge originally a Latin verb, but could well have been an appropriate one for 'I shop' had the Romans so decided. The phrase I attribute first to Lesslie Newbigin.

3   Craig Bartholomew, in Bartholomew and Moritz, *Christ and Consumerism*, p6.

4   See Richard Foster's related comment: 'We must clearly understand that the lust for affluence in contemporary society is psychotic'; from *Celebration of Discipline: The Path to Spiritual Growth*, Hodder & Stoughton, 1980, p70.

5   An excellent practical introduction to this issue can be found in Richard Foster, *Money, Sex and Power: The Challenge of the Disciplined Life*, Hodder & Stoughton, 1985. A more serious biblical theology can be found in Craig Blomberg, *Neither Poverty nor Riches: A Biblical Theology of Material Possessions*, Apollos/InterVarsity Press, 1999.

6   Dorling Kindersley was bought out by Pearson plc in May 2000 after making a $40 million loss, of which $22 million was due to the overproduction of a *Star Wars* book.

7   Research undertaken by Prof. Paul Williams of Southampton University. 'Weekend Money', *The Times*, 4 Dec 1999.

8   Jonathan Sacks develops this theme in *The Politics of Hope*, Jonathan Cape, 1997: see, for example, pp115,176.

9   Peter Berger, Brigitte Berger and Hansfried Kellner, *The Homeless Mind: Modernization and Consciousness*, Penguin, 1974, p77.

10 I owe this point to Craig Bartholomew, in Bartholomew and Moritz, *Christ and Consumerism*, p6.

11 Several stores opened even on Christmas Day in 2000.

12 See especially Zygmunt Bauman, *Intimations of Postmodernity*, Routledge, 1992, pp224–225. Bauman is a leading sociologist who perceives consumerism to be 'a very central category' in understanding contemporary society. He accuses it of 'duplicity' both in promising that all can be happy if they are free to exercise consumer choice, and in pretending that freedom is to be equated with consumerism.

13 Craig Bartholomew, '*Consuming God's word: biblical interpretation and consumerism*' in Bartholomew and Moritz, *Christ and Consumerism*, pp81–99.

14 Rick Warren, *The Purpose Driven Church: Growth Without Compromising Your Message and Mission*, Zondervan, 1995, p395.

15 This is not the whole story concerning the growth of employment of church workers. It also has to do with the increasing professionalisation of standards and the growing bureaucratisation of society.

16 See Michael Griffiths, *The Example of Jesus*, Hodder & Stoughton, 1985, p43.

17 For practical help, see Richard Foster, *Freedom of Simplicity*, Triangle/SPCK, 1981.

Chapter 6

The challenge of consumerism: A matter of choice?

Anna Robbins

'When you've got cheese, you've got choice!' proclaimed the old cheddar adverts I used to see on television. Consumerist patterns of economic behaviour throughout the Western world suggest that the individual is empowered by the proliferation of choice; so much so that the purchase of cheese isn't heralded for the benefit it might bring to your culinary creations but for your empowering as the individual consumer. Your choice is what is important – *your* decision, *your* needs, *your* wants. It's all about you and not about cheese at all.

The truth is, despite living in what seems to be a ruggedly individualistic society, our lives are virtually intertwined with others every moment of every day. Even the most innocuous activities bind us together with the rest of humanity in ways that we often overlook.

In my cupboard at the moment I have five types of rice – Italian arborio, Thai fragrant, Indian basmati, long grain and brown wild. They come from five different countries on three different continents. I can hardly imagine the number of lives that have invested time and energy producing a bag of rice for my shelf, from the farm labourer, to the factory processor, to the machine operators who printed the plastic bag in which it arrived in my supermarket. Yet sometimes I cannot help but think of whether all those people will enjoy as healthy and as happy a meal as I will tonight.

If I cannot eat everything I have cooked, I will throw the leftovers away. Is it possible that some of the same hands that harvested my rice will be picking through a rubbish heap looking to salvage something that might be exchanged for a meal? The social imbalance of consumerism is starkly reflected on bin day in my neighbourhood. Last week there were piles of old exercise bicycles, old beds and old lawn mowers: many of these items still functioned but had been replaced with newer, more desirable models. And they were thrown into the back of a rubbish truck and taken away. I wished they could have been taken to the tip I once saw in Guatemala, where tens of thousands of people live and eke out an existence from the smoking rubbish piles. Our garbage may have given a few of them a new lease on life. Instead, it will mark a shrinking green landscape with virtually indestructible materials, or be burned, releasing more pollution into the atmosphere than was necessary to produce the stuff in the first place.

If I cannot eat everything I have cooked, I will throw the leftovers away.

When I think about such things, I confess I feel almost paralysed by the overwhelming complexities of the global economic system and the burden of my privileged position within it. It is too difficult to wade through the issues and find the truth beneath the layers of investment and ownership. I can't accept the responsibility of knowing where everything I buy comes from, who makes it and whether or not its production was based on human or environmental exploitation. It is so much easier to try to forget such things and get on with the business of my own life, serving the kingdom of God from my little corner of the world. If I feel particularly guilty on any given day, I can always set aside a few extra quid for the most recent disaster and relief appeal. But the questions nag. Is this good enough? Am I meeting the obligation of servanthood that belongs to me as a recipient of grace from the One who has saved me, into a community that stretches from the greatest to the least? Am I really being defined by discipleship and not consumerism, as Derek Tidball challenged in the previous chapter?

These kinds of questions also plagued many evangelicals in the nineteenth century. At that time, it was a few of the wealthy from town and country, and some committed city dwellers, who were moved to alleviate the suffering of many in industrial England who were forced to labour for a meagre existence in those 'dark satanic mills'. A wave of philanthropy surged through society, and committed Christians were often found at the forefront of a movement which began to transform British society so that the basic needs of most would be met, and people could begin to hope for a better future for themselves and their children.

We don't even have to go that far to find people with profound needs. We can see them all around us, sometimes on a daily basis.

The global situation today bears many similarities with the situations of our past, though problems exist on a far grander scale. This is a complex matter, but it is clear that deeply offensive levels of poverty still exist among our neighbours. They are not seen by us on a daily basis, walking through our cities and labouring in our factories. And yet, they are only a few hours' travelling distance away, labouring in appalling conditions – if they can find work at all – producing goods they will never afford to use, for people in a wealthy land they will never see. We don't even have to go that far to find people with profound needs. We can see them all around us, sometimes on a daily basis – people whose circumstances or ability to cope with life has left them vulnerable and marginalised. But the level of global disparity is particularly appalling and difficult to comprehend. The desire, the responsibility, to do something to bridge the gap between rich and poor weighs heavily upon me as a disciple of Christ who seeks to be defined by the compassion of discipleship and not the callousness of consumerism.

If we thought the situation was complicated enough already, it gets worse. Globalisation is the new reality, **Globalisation is the new reality, giving rise to the universalisation of economy and culture which is, for the most part, Western and consumerist.** giving rise to the universalisation of economy and culture which is, for the most part, Western and consumerist in nature. The potentially rich contribution of diverse cultures to this mosaic is turned into a culturally-commodifying billboard. Traditional Mayan belts become dog collars and leashes; Tibetan chants become rock music; uninterpreted Oriental script adorns furniture, drapes and tableware.

To be fair, this commodification of culture happens in the opposite direction as well, but the harmful effects of global consumerism ought not to be overlooked.[1] The desired quality of life is displayed worldwide through television and advertising, and local cultures are compromised in their desire to conform to a standard that offers the promise of the good life. But is it the good life which is really on offer? Or is it the hollow shell of an unattainable image which beckons attention and demands loyalty? It may be unfortunate if my next-door neighbour purchases a particular brand of cigarettes/jeans/softdrinks because she thinks they will make her fit in with her peer group. But it is tragic if my far-away neighbour, with scarce resources, is being bombarded with the message that the purchase of those same cigarettes/jeans/softdrinks will deliver the kind of lifestyle she longs for.

In light of this reality, I no longer feel only the burden of my privileged position as a citizen of a wealthy country; I also feel totally insignificant in a system that finds my banked life savings as a paltry investment in multinational companies with annual turnovers in excess of the GDP of some countries, even some 'developed' countries. The world's largest MNCs possess economies a quarter of the size of Canada's GDP, and an eighth of the size of Britain's. Software producers are developing new methods of marketing which demand not only loyalty but technological enslavement to their particular product development. I am only a pawn in this vast scheme, and a pretty insignificant one at that.

The more I consider these issues, the more overwhelmed I feel by the tension between the responsibility that is mine as a privileged member of global society, and the limitations that prevent my actions from having any apparent influence. If there is nothing I can do, then I might as well resign myself to life as part of a consumer culture and focus my efforts on the spiritual side of life, longing for the day when Christ will come again and set everything right. Or, if I am called to do something, anything, then maybe I should give everything up and go to live and minister with those who struggle against the oppression of poverty and injustice. Perhaps my social salvation lies in identification with the needy of this world, who are not counted among the power brokers of exploitative consumer culture.

Yet neither of these answers seems completely satisfactory. Perhaps what I need to do is take stock of my options and think about what possible attitudes I might have to these issues. Then I may decide how best to respond, if it seems a response is necessary.

So what are my choices?

A 'health and wealth' gospel

Bert thinks that material benefits are a sign of God's blessing. He believes he has been rewarded for his faithfulness to God with the large house, two cars and tasteful art collection that he owns. He anticipates that, as he continues to serve God, he will continue to acquire more luxuries. After all, he decides, God didn't make all those diamonds for the devil's folks!

Bert has surrendered to the materialism of a consumer culture and defines his life by it. His life in Christ is generally oriented around what he is able to acquire, without concern for the consequences for others and the environment. His Christian compassion for other people is manifested in a desire that they come to know the riches that might be theirs if they worship Christ and pray for material blessings as he has done. Bert knows little of self-sacrifice and costly discipleship. As far as the 'less fortunate' are concerned, he believes it must be their own fault somehow. You just can't help some people, and giving money away to people in other countries is akin to waste; it will probably end up in the hands of corrupt officials, and those who need it will never see it anyway. Why bother? *Pass the caviar, please.*

A radical lifestyle

Jim used to be an 'average' Christian who grew up in the church as part of a middle-class family. As he got older, he found that his Christian background offered him little by way of appreciating the struggle of the world's oppressed people, and the fragile balance that exists in God's creation. Jim felt misunderstood when he challenged his church to be more involved in these issues, which he believes carry eternal significance. When he encountered a group of like-minded people, they decided to share a house which they adapted to employ alternative technologies, and where they shared all resources and responsibilities. Jim considers himself to be on the fringe of the Christian church, but thinks this kind of lifestyle commitment is the only way to live out his Christian convictions with integrity. Some people pity Jim, and consider him and his friends to be drop-outs from society. More recently, he has gone to India to live and work in a poor urban area. He believes that if every Christian did something similar, the world would be a different, and better, place. *Pass the peace, man.*

Worlds divided

Jane is a typical, hard-working Christian who lives and works in a large town. She saves for the things she needs and wants. She does not have an extravagant lifestyle, but neither is she often faced with the reality of poverty. It concerns her when she visits the city and sees so many people in need, and she is always unsure what to do when somebody on a street in town asks for money. She wants to help but in ways that will be most effective. She gives regularly to charity through her church, and through other organisations working in Britain and in other countries. Being concerned for other people is something that comes naturally to her, and something which she thinks ought to come naturally to all people regardless of their beliefs. But Jane doesn't see how being a Christian really changes the way she understands her life as a consumer; nor does she make any connection between her life as a Christian and the facts of economic and cultural globalisation. She never thinks about where the money in her bank or pension account is actually invested, or where her clothes are manufactured. Feeling somewhat powerless, she prays and waits for the day when this world will pass away. Then what is now defined as 'spiritual' will comprise all reality. The material will be gone, with all of its exploitation and inequality. For this reason, Jane finds value and comfort in keeping these realms of her life more or less separate. *Just passin' through.*

Charity

Joe lives life with an open hand. He sees everything good that comes into his life as a blessing to be passed on. He is always ready to receive what comes his way and to give when there is a need. He has a good income and a large inheritance, which enables him to be extremely generous. Because of his Christian beliefs, he lives modestly in light of his means, though possessing more things than anyone could need. He researches his charities so that he knows how his money will be used most effectively. A number of organisations have honoured him with awards and dinners for his charitable giving. Joe finds nothing more satisfying than giving money to an individual or a group and suggesting ways they might use it to make their lives and work more productive. For him, it is gratifying to lend a financial hand to somebody in need. Joe is thankful to be in a position to help other people. He is especially proud of the new rehabilitation wing at the hospital which bears his name on a plaque near the entrance. *I want to pass it on.*

Justice

Tara believes that this world is full of sin and we will always have the poor with us. But she also believes that God's grace makes it possible for the frontiers of sin to be pushed back and bring a certain degree of relief from oppression, poverty and suffering. She is convinced that she has a participatory role in this, though she will be plagued constantly by the tensions between her life in this world and her life in the kingdom of God. She doesn't want these to be exclusive realms, but she recognises the difference between them. What she seeks is balance – a balance between what is possible because of grace, and what is necessary because of sin. She lives a 'charitable' life, but is also involved with other people at home and overseas in practical projects that attempt to empower whole communities to make decisions about their future. As she engages in these activities, she is aware that she embodies as many limitations as those around her. Therefore, everything she does is for the glory of God. She prays that he will give the church courage to strive toward fulfilment of his promises in Christ. She recognises that while she participates in his work, he alone is able to bring it to full consummation. *Lord, do not pass us by.*

Making a choice

It is difficult to know how to choose between these options, but it is clear that the best response lies with an approach that most closely resembles a biblical conception of justice. This kind of justice grows out of living in right relationship with those around us, and is characterised by our *vertical* relationship with God. The righteousness of a right relationship with God does not lie in our ability to love and serve our Creator, but in his grace demonstrated on the cross of Christ. Out of his own action of self-sacrifice, God has set us right with himself. And the outworking of this righteous relationship with our Creator God is the *horizontal* relationship of justice with the rest of creation. This means not only giving people their due – their fair share – but treating them with the same attitude of self-sacrifice and love that set us right with God in the first place. Such an attitude comes to us as a gift of God's Spirit and not from our own moral resources.

But this doesn't let us off the hook! A biblical conception of justice teaches us to recognise our responsibility for one another out of a sense of gratitude to God for the love he has given to us. This will work out in the lives of Christians as a desire that all might come to know his saving grace; as compassion in the face of physical and emotional suffering; as concern for the voiceless of society; as a commitment to value and nurture the gifts of creation so that they are protected and properly managed for the benefit of everyone, thus giving glory to God.

A biblical conception of justice recognises the presence of sin that permeates every human activity, but it does not accept sin as the last word. It accepts human responsibility for the structures we have created, even though those structures seem at times to take on a life of their own. No matter how complicated life may seem, biblical justice believes that God's justice is present in the world through his grace. Biblical justice supports the idea that what we do in this life matters, and has eternal consequences. Such a concept enables us to make decisions about how we can view and act in the world without feeling defeated or taking upon ourselves a false responsibility to bring in God's final justice. It keeps us ever watchful, ever hopeful, ever humble and ever resourceful.

I confess that several of the examples described above have appealed to me at various times of my life for different reasons. But it is one which focuses on God's justice which seems to embrace rather than abandon the ambiguities and ethical tensions of life in today's world. Maybe the answer lies in not being at home in consumer culture, or *any* culture. And yet Christ is present in every culture, speaking out of it and speaking into it. Perhaps the fact that I often feel so uncomfortable about some of these aspects of my cultural skin is a sign that something is right even while it's wrong. After all, Christ embraced the pain and suffering of this world. His was not an easy answer and he made the hardest choice. Will we?

Endnote

1   This is documented in several articles in David Howes (ed), *Cross-cultural Consumption: Global Markets, Local Realities*, Routledge, 1996.

Chapter 7

The challenge of progress: From modernity to post-modernity and beyond

Graham McFarlane

> Make them as happy as is good for them.
> But that's a hard one, for I have to add: consultation
> with their wishes;
> Which is the crevice that lets Progress in.
> If we could only stop the Progress somewhere,
> At a good point for pliant permanence,
> Where Madison attempted to arrest it.
>
> *(Robert Frost)*[1]

The notion of 'progress' lies at the very heart of the biblical vision for humanity and the wider creation. Its origins are located in Genesis 1...

> God blessed them and said to them, 'Be fruitful and increase in number; fill the earth and subdue it. Rule over the fish of the sea and the birds of the air and over every living creature that moves on the ground.'
>
> *(Genesis 1:28)*

...and are reiterated in Genesis 17, in God's covenant with Abram...

> ...the Lord appeared to him and said, 'I am the God
> Almighty; walk before me and be blameless. I will
> confirm my covenant between me and you and will
> greatly increase your numbers...'
>
> *(Genesis 17:1–2)*

...and its fulfilment is hinted at in the great promise of
Revelation...

> I heard a loud voice from the throne saying, 'Now the
> dwelling of God is with men, and will live with them.
> They will be his people, and God himself will be with
> them and be their God.'
>
> *(Revelation 21:3)*

Thus the golden thread of progress weaves through
the narrative of creation, covenant and re-creation. It
attests to the creature's *hope* and the Creator's *intention*:
that one day the creature and Creator will commune
without barrier or hindrance.

Traditionally, the human journey through time from
past to present and on to the future has been identified
in terms of 'loss' – a fall from what was meant to be to
what now is. Progress, in this sense, is measured against
an idealised vision of humankind's beginning. However,
such an interpretation is too one-dimensional: it
embraces only one aspect of a wider story. According to
the Judeao–Christian narrative, progress is located not
only in recovering what has been lost, but also in moving
forward towards what has not yet even been discovered
– what is still unknown, unexplored, unexperienced.

It is this latter definition of progress that lies at the
heart of Christian faith. Words such as 'pilgrim', 'perse-

verance', 'striving', promise', all communicate a sense of incompleteness – the 'not-yet', the 'not-having-arrived'. In short, Christians have a sense of being determined not simply by their past, but much more by what is still to come. In theological language, this is described as their *eschatological* hope, a hope located beyond the immediate self. Such a hope resides in what we identify as 'the end' (*eschaton*).

The perception that we are conditioned not by our origins (which are tainted by the fall and sin) but by what lies at 'the end' is an important one for the Christian identity. Any form of progress is to be understood in relation to something that lies beyond ourselves. In addition, the greater our belief in something beyond ourselves, the more confident will we be that progress is actually a sensible thing to pursue. Consequently, it is the the nature of what lies beyond that ultimately determines the kind of expectation we have of progress.

The question is, 'What is it that lies beyond?'

The progress of Western culture

For the most part, Western history has been concerned with the pursuit of truth. This quest has gone hand-in-hand with the growth and predominance of Christianity. Truth, reason, science and knowledge as we know them in the West have, until recently, been founded on a Christian world-view.

At the same time, the pursuit of truth has taken place within a wider world-view which took for granted the belief in an ordered universe, where knowledge correlated to notions of reason, application and discovery.

This ordered universe made it possible both to make discovery and to interpret its meaning – twin criteria which determined our sense of progress. Over time, human progress created its own cumulative body of knowledge and tradition, which eventually became the yardstick by which progress could be measured. Without the past, without memory, without tradition, there can be no sense of progress. There can be no understanding that boundaries are being pushed, that knowledge is being expanded: instead, there can only be innovation.

The dogma of a reliable Creator and creation ... was overturned and replaced by an alternative dogma.

It would be true to say that this pursuit of a progressive body of knowledge was the generally held goal within the Christian West for nearly one and a half millennia. The world was fixed by an orderly Creator in such a way that discovery was possible: the world could be *known*. As a consequence, this knowledge spawned a body of tradition as well as faith in a certain future. In the pre-modern world, then, progress was necessarily connected with the continuation of what lay before.

All this was to change, however, in the seventeenth century. The dogma of a reliable Creator and creation, which had undergirded Western belief in progress, was overturned and replaced by an alternative dogma. (No society can prosper, no society can exist without some form of dogma, some 'seemingly good' set of beliefs). It was the French philosopher René Descartes who moved the centre of thinking away from a reliable creation, the known world, and back to the person who does the thinking, the knowing subject. With this massive change of direction, Western culture underwent a significant cultural shift: it experienced a form of Enlightenment.

We could describe this as the *secularisation* of the idea of progress *en masse*. From now on, it was no longer God who determined the rate of progress, but human beings.

In Enlightenment circles, fundamental to the notion of progress was the flight from religion to autonomy. Over time the church no longer played a dominant role within society. God was ultimately disenfranchised. Truth, reality and knowledge were no longer accepted solely on the grounds of religious faith but, increasingly, on the basis of human reason. Thus began the Western preoccupation with *foundations* – knowledge that was totally reliable, unchallengeable and universal. The search was on for a body of truth which did not require any 'leap of faith' or fawning to a superior, religious authority. Progress was increasingly located within the realm of *human* possibility. Scientific knowledge became the arbiter of progress – albeit in relation to God, at least to start with. However, this divine-human relationship was curtailed a century later by the philosophers David Hume, in Britain, and Immanuel Kant, in Germany. Human reason was now viewed separately from divine revelation. Human progress was no longer determined in relation to divine criteria. It had 'grown up' and no longer needed a divine guardian.

Since miracles were a violation of nature, people reasoned, it followed that they could not be true.

Thus, by the mid-eighteenth century, the notion of 'reasonableness' had become the criterion for what could and could not be accepted both in nature and in religion. Take, for example, the argument concerning miracles: since miracles were a violation of nature, people reasoned, it followed that they could not be true. Instead, miracles had to be interpreted in 'non-natural' ways – as myth, or as primitive ways of expressing what we would now use science to explain. Nonetheless, reasonableness for some, including Kant, still depended on some universal revelation.

By the nineteenth century, the notion of progress became aligned, in the minds of many, with two key aspects of Western culture – *economics* and *industrialisation*. Throughout the age of Enlightenment, there was a deep belief in the relationship between progress and economic growth. Thinkers such as Voltaire argued for the essential link between commerce, freedom and progress. In the nineteenth century, this economic belief was coupled with the massive expansion of industrial activity and growth – so much so that, by the mid-twentieth century, it was simply assumed that industrial and technological progress would bring economic progress.

The Darwinian belief in the biological progress of the human species only served to reinforce the hope placed in the notion of progress itself.

Human beings had the ability, it was argued, to create 'heaven on earth' by means of either the socialisation of technology (Western communism), or through the democratisation of market forces (Western capitalism). In addition, as Western capitalism became expressed increasingly through a consumerist culture, any sense of progress had to outwork itself in terms of material prosperity and progressively higher standards of living. Progress, then, became attached to technological and material success, and material success both fed, and was fed, by industry, banking and technology.

Such an economic notion of progress was sustained by the underlying cultural belief of biological progress, that human beings had the potential to improve themselves by means of *natural selection*. The Darwinian belief in the biological progress of the human species only served to reinforce the hope placed in the notion of progress itself. Such hope was soon to prove misplaced in the light of two world wars, during which the human creature so vividly demonstrated its capacity for destruction.

However, any disappointment was to be short-lived. The notion of biological progress soon came to be replaced by a much more material expression: the belief in progress relocated itself in the Western capacity to *consume*. In such a cycle, popular culture assumes that the more and the better one consumes, the more and the better one is. It is, admittedly, an argument that leads nowhere, but nevertheless it has come to be widely believed. At the heart of this belief is a conflict between the ways in which the origins and workings of creation are perceived. The modernist world-view, in its techno-logical form, reduces all things to the capacity of the machine. The faith placed in a weekly lottery gives evidence to this cultural dogma: a machine becomes the means of determining the destiny of the lucky few in a manner similar to the fate of the three-eyed, talking aliens in *Toy Story*, who wait their turn to be picked out of the coin-machine to find a new life. This new life, however, comes with a cost:

> And the machines say, laughing
> up what would have been sleeves
> in the old days: 'We are at
> your service.' 'Take us', we cry,
> 'to the places that are far off
> from yourselves.' And so they do
> at a price that is the alloy in
> the thought that we can do without them.

(R S Thomas, 'Fuel', *Collected Poems 1945–1990*, Phoenix Giant, 1996)

What, then, are the fruits of Western progress once it has been aligned with economic and technological growth? At the centre of the present cultural shift from modernity to postmodernity, we can identify a growing cultural malaise, the evidence of which can be seen in our individualism, our sense of being overwhelmed by life, our boredom and our collective self-interest. On the one hand, our social and economic goals have been increasingly met. Yet they fail to fulfil the needs and expectations that generated them, and we experience the consequences. Childhood and adult obesity become more the norm as our taste buds become more and more desensitised, and our wallets feed newer and more refined palates. Pornography becomes an increasingly popular diversion in a culture that, having achieved emancipation, finds itself bored with its freedom. The promise of progress proclaimed by modernism has ultimately not been delivered:

> Things fall apart; the centre cannot hold;
> Mere anarchy is loosed upon the world,
> The blood-dimmed tide is loosed, and everywhere
> The ceremony of innocence is drowned;
> The best lack all conviction, while the worst
> Are full of passionate intensity.
>
> (W B Yeats, 'The Second Coming',
> Collected Poems of W B Yeats, Macmillan, 1971)

If we look at the individual birthed by modern progress, we see an unstable, rather fragile expression of humanity. In the past our humanity was identified in terms of relationships, geography and occupation – all relatively fixed identities. Today, however, the modern individual has progressed into a more vapid and abstract entity. Relationships become disposable due to the fluid nature of modern culture. Occupations are increasingly a means to a consumerist end: *Tesco ergo sum* for the masses, *Harvey Nichols ergo sum* for the cognoscenti. The modern individual has brought with him an unprecedented cultural crisis in terms of both self and collective identity. As Zygmunt Bauman so aptly puts it: 'At the heart of sociality is the loneliness of the moral person'.[2] Who am I if I cannot have my consumerist identity? What is the essential 'me'? With whom am I relating? On what grounds do we meet, coexist, relate? Contemporary progress, it would appear, has brought about much uncertainty and insecurity.

Dallas Willard sees a more humorous side to this somewhat sad scenario:

> Most of us as individuals, and world society as a whole, live at high speed and often with no clue to whether we are flying upside down or right side up. Indeed, we are haunted by a strong suspicion that there may be no difference.
>
> (Dallas Willard, The Divine Conspiracy, Fount, 1998, p7)

This insecurity is fed by a burgeoning range of consumer choice which has led us, as a culture, to the point of saturation. We are overwhelmed by the sheer volume of opportunities: what to eat, what to buy, what identity to assume, who to be. As our capacity to consume increases, so too does our ability to homogenise our various choices. What was once a luxury, a rare treat, something to hope for, is now viewed as common and mundane. And, over time, this cultivates a culture of boredom, as we become conditioned toward the new in our increasing attempts to dull the ache brought on by such boredom.

Here lies the cultural myth – that salvation consists of the capacity to meet our need to overcome the boredom in our lives. Thus the consumerist cycle is completed by the 'salvation myth': if only we improve, are better educated, more in control, then we will be happier and more fulfilled. We will be saved! Of course, this doctrine of salvation requires constant access to goods. As Wauzzinski wryly comments, 'Because optimists find their remedies for all of life's problems in technology, they must create, then saturate culture, with technical objects'.[3]

The biblical story of creation, fall and redemption introduces a radical definition of the concept of progress unlike any of its secular equivalents.

Perhaps the ultimate expression of progress gone awry is not our capacity to consume goods but each other. The progress promised by seventeenth-century optimism came to flower in the Age of Catastrophe.[4] The great messianic claim, that progress would bring peace and prosperity, flies in the face of modern Western history. The First World War dashed the ideals of nineteenth-century philosophers, and the Second World War put an end to any residual belief that the previous war was an unfortunate blot on an otherwise clean sheet. The subsequent Cold War between the superpowers from opposite sides of the same 'progressive' coin, simply sealed the fate of any grand anthropology in which swords and spears would be melted down into ploughshares and pruning hooks.

The subversion of progress

Too often Christians have sided with secular under-standings of progress. Indeed, at times it would almost appear that Christianity has claimed the patent on 'progress'. Whether it be the Crusades, the Reformation, Mom's Apple Pie, Rule Britannia or wannabe John-Lewis lookalikes, Christians constantly seek to align themselves with 'progressive' elements within society. The question is, 'Why'? Is this a complete aberration on their part? Or is it just something that comes with the Western cultural package? Perhaps it is neither. Perhaps the answer lies in the opening statement of this chapter, that the notion of progress is central to the Judeao-Christian faiths.

Indeed, if you think about it, there is no other option. It is almost impossible to live without some sense of progression. Movement, in what-ever direction, is the essence of any biological life. We either move forward or backward. Even standing still will alter the ecosystem – it leads to stagnation. We either have positive progress or negative progress, which may lead to life or death. This is a biological, social and personal fact. Therefore, the question is not whether progress exists, but what kind of progress is it?

The Christian notion of progress turns on one word – 'repentance'.

At this point the biblical response kicks in. The biblical story of creation, fall and redemption introduces a radical definition of the concept of progress unlike any of its secular equivalents. The reason for this is simple: as far as the Christian Scriptures are concerned, *there is no positive sense of progress within the created realm*. Why? Because, as the apostle Paul reminds us, as a result of humanity's misuse of their God-given authority, the whole of creation has come under God's curse, and suffers as a result (Rom 8:20–22). As such, creation simply does not have the capacity for self-improvement. It is unable, in and of itself, to do anything. It can only hope for the coming of that by which its transformation can be realised.

And so we arrive at the central point of the whole Christian gospel. This transformation will only come through relationship with Jesus Christ. It is only his creative and transforming presence that offers any hope of progress for human beings and for the rest of creation. It is when redeemed human beings reflect the true human, Jesus Christ, that creation catches a glimpse of its future glory. As such, the Christian notion of progress turns on one word – 'repentance'. Only to the degree that we turn, collectively and individually, away from false and pretentious notions of what will or will not save us, will we be able to experience true progress, the progress offered by the incarnate God.

The progress described in Christian Scripture is the movement from death to life, from darkness to light, from fear to security, from illness to wholeness, from condemnation to acceptance, from guilt to innocence, from loneliness to community, from self-interest to love. It is a 'John 3:16' kind of progress which assumes the responsibility of the creature to respond to the Creator's action in Christ Jesus. It demands a subversion of all other pretensions to position, power and progress. It is the collective stance of individuals who have experienced God's love in Christ, who have seen something of the Creator's glory, who have said, 'That's for me!'. It is the subversive attitude that sees beyond one's own ego towards another way of being. Progress, in this sense, is the kingdom ethic of giving rather than keeping, losing rather than saving, being last rather than first, self-denying rather than self-fulfilling, dying rather than living. It is to walk to the beat of a different drum, to laugh at the false salvation packages on offer, to live by faith, to be assured of what is hoped for, certain of what has not yet been seen.

Why? Because the resurrection of Jesus Christ – from a blood-whipped, back-torn, nail-splintered, back-breaking death, to a transformed, death-defying, spectacularly new kind of life – screams out, against all other doctrines of progress. This is the only kind of progress worth putting all your money on. It defies what all other doctrines of progress seek to avoid, our greatest fear both individually and collectively – it defies death. Only Jesus Christ embodies the ultimate form of progress: the kind that moves creation beyond its own terminal existence to a new and non-stop existence. This is resurrection, this is eternal life, this is the kingdom of God. And it is only found in Jesus Christ.

Endnotes

1   'How hard it is to keep from being King when it's in you and in the situation', *The Poetry of Robert Frost*, Jonathan Cape, 1976).

2   Zygmunt Bauman, *Postmodern Ethics*, Blackwell, 1993, p240.

3   Robert A Wauzzinski, *'Technological optimism'*, *Perspectives on Science and Christian Faith*, September 1996, vol 48. p150.

4   Jürgen Moltmann, 'Progress and abyss: Remembering the future of the modern world', in *Review and Expositor*, 2000, vol 97, p306.

Chapter 8

The challenge of progress: Will computers take over?

Conrad Gempf

Two images

When I consider computer technology from a Christian perspective, my mind involuntarily shoots sideways to two images only semi-related to the topic. The first is the more obscure of the two: an image of my father at the seaside. My dad was the work ethic incarnate. Even his recreation was couched, although with deliberate playfulness, in terms of duty and struggle. We didn't just go swimming or play in the surf, rather, it was our (mock serious) duty to fight the waves. As if enough active resistance by enough holidaymakers could prevent the tide from coming in. All your sandcastles are safe.

The second image is more straightforward: that of the car. *Wired* magazine once printed an article by Hans Moravec of Carnagie-Mellon University. In it, he argued that before the end of the twenty-first century, intelligent machines would more or less take over the world. In reply, the editors received a marvellous letter from a reader:

> ...As for intelligent machines taking over, a machine does not have to be intelligent to conquer the world; it

> merely has to be desirable. We've already lost one war
> to a synthetic species–the automobile–that has killed
> over a million people, occupied all of our cities [in
> most cases causing the original human inhabitants to
> reshape those cities to fit the convenience of cars]...
> and exacts crushing taxes in [natural] resources, wealth
> and time from over half the planet.
>
> *(Grant Thompson, letter to the editor,*
> *Wired UK, 2.01, January 1996, p12)*

These images illustrate two major points: standing up to some things just doesn't work; and technology is not neutral.

It has often been claimed that all technology is neutral. It is hard to argue with the literal truth of the old US pro-gun lobby slogan: 'Guns don't kill people; people kill people.' According to science fiction, even nuclear bombs (in the right hands) could bring great benefits to humanity. How else would you destroy or divert meteors from collision paths with Earth? It's not the item, it's the misuse of the item. One could argue that *cars* didn't murder the high street; *people* preferring to drive and park at the huge shopping centres and malls killed the high street. One could even say that cars don't pollute; people driving cars pollute.

Not neutral

Technology is not neutral, but neither is it either good or evil. The morality of technology is a morality of trade-offs. It is difficult to conceive of loving uses of anti-personnel land mines, but there may be some. On the other hand, even apparently innocent technologies have their misuses: where would the pornography industry be without photography?

But evaluating the trade-offs is not only difficult, it is probably impossible. There have been huge conferences on the benefits and dangers of the computer revolution but, standing as we do at the infancy (or at least toddler-hood) of that emerging technology, we are in no position to truly evaluate it.

Can you imagine a conference on the automobile when that industry was in *its* infancy? People of the day did seem to comprehend some of the benefits, although the most compelling reasons for using a car seemed to centre on fashion and the dis-advantages of using horses. The dangers were either poorly understood, miscon-ceived or totally unforeseen. If you travel too much faster than a galloping horse, one scientist warned, the air would be sucked past you at such a rate that you would be unable to breathe and would die of asphyxiation at the steering wheel. Not much attention was paid to any possible long-term effects of emissions, nor to the problems of drunk driving and other major killers.

> How could you have warned people ... of the increased stress levels caused by having to commute by car through traffic day in, day out?

No one could have predicted the social effects on communities either. How could you have warned people at the turn of the last century of the increased stress levels caused by having to commute by car through traffic day in, day out? The same people who listened attentively to the predictions of high-speed respiratory failure would mock you if you tried to tell them about 'road rage'. The idea that scientific advances in transportation could be the cause of turning rational human beings into crazed beasts would have struck them as ludicrous. Nor would scientifically testing a handful of cars in a closed environment have yielded useful information about the changes to society or the scale of pollution.

What makes us think that we can do any better at predicting the effects of computer technology today? Like the car, computer technology is poised on the brink of being everywhere. Internet sites, email addresses and boxes that you recognise as computers are only the tip of a much larger iceberg. Alan Turing and his code-breaking companions of the war years would have done anything for the computing power wasted in your new washer-dryer. The coming ubiquity of computer technology is not neutral. It will change things irreversibly. It will shift the balances of power and possibilities in myriad ways. It's not surprising that we can't foresee them. Hundreds of thousands of the most innovative minds of the coming generation will be bending their energies toward discovering those opportunities, inventing those possibilities and shifting those balances.

What should we look for?

Clearly it would be arrogant to think that we could do anything more than *begin* to anticipate the work of all those minds, yet some contours of the future use of computer technology should occur to us as things to watch and be concerned about. The lessons of the past show us that some of these may turn out to be mere bogeymen, like the asphyxiation threat of motor vehicles. However, we need to remain alert for dangers we have not anticipated.

If there's one area of computer technology that Christians have been alerted to, it is the issue of pornography. While pornography in print and online should be a major concern for Christians, the Internet poses few dangers not already present in our current system of newsagents. Pornographers are not, on the whole, known for their philanthropy. When they move from magazines to web sites, they are unlikely to begin offering their wares for free. At present the only way to get money from someone over the Internet is via a credit card transaction. Thus, while people can acquire printed pornography by visiting a newsagent where they are not known and can use the anonymous payment of cash, it is harder – not easier – to purchase pornography anonymously through the Internet. There are erotic images available for free online, but it's just as easy for consumers to acquire such material using a VCR to capture late-night broadcast films as use a computer to download pictures off the Internet.

The 'danger' of pornography tends to be emphasised by large organisations who would like to turn the Internet from a 'many to many' communication–sharing system into a 'few to many' broadcast-type system. They will argue that, because of dangers like pornography, only those who meet certain conditions should be allowed to 'broadcast' on the new media, and someone (namely, themselves) should be in charge of controlling who can share what to whom (and be paid for the privilege). As we see with television, however, when the medium is controlled by those whose motives are profit, then they have a duty to their shareholders to broadcast whatever sells. Privatised television companies have, if anything, *increased* the amount of sexual material on view. There's little reason to believe the handling of a controlled Internet would be very different.

Not unrelated to this is the issue of privacy. For years we have feared being viewed as mere statistics. With databases, 'customer cards' and computerised tills, this has become more of a danger than ever before. *Time* magazine (25 August 1997) quoted Carol Lane, a 'Paid Internet Searcher', as saying, 'Beginning with no more than your name and address, I can find out what you do for a living, the names and ages of your spouse and children, what kind of car you drive, the value of your house and how much tax you pay on it.' Our purchases can be tracked and used to place us into demographic groups ready to be targeted for laser-guided adverts. Like electronic Sherlock Holmeses, data-collection agencies build up a profile of who you are and what you are likely to be tempted into buying on the basis of the electronic footprints you leave on the cyberlandscape. Purchase a dog lead at a large department store, and the supermarket branch of the chain will start mailing you dog-food adverts. Purchase enough 'convenience meals' at the supermarket and watch the ads for microwave ovens start flooding through the letterbox.

Even if you are 'one in a million', there are hundreds just like you online.

There are also a cluster of issues surrounding the idea of community and isolation. Despite books like Howard Rheingold's *Virtual Community*, and numerous popular anecdotes of vicars 'talking' to motorcycle gang-members online, once computers and email are out of the 'hobby' stage of their development, they will join the telephone and motorcar in allowing us to spend more time finding and socialising with people we already know or are inclined to like, and less time with people we don't know or who are unlike us. The point-and-

'clique' world of online discussions tends toward specialisation. Even if you are 'one in a million', there are hundreds just like you online. As more people get 'wired', the specialty groups get narrower and narrower. At one point, you might have talked to other people who liked Christian rock music, and found out that although no one else liked your favourite band, there were other bands they thought you would find worth a listen. Now there are whole discussion groups focussed on your favourite band in which thirty emailed messages come through every day. You won't hear of the other bands. You needn't spend much time at all with anyone who doesn't already agree with you.

A curious trend to be watched is something I call 'dematerialism' – despite the popular perception, the computer era is not a new type of materialism. Manufacturers and salesmen would like you to believe that you need the latest hardware. But, for the most part, the emphasis is off the hardware – the stuff – and on the information. Part of a wider trend in society, you see this in the move away from manufacturing and into service industries. This has long been the case with parts of the entertainment business, such as the BBC: your licence fee brings you signal-patterns of information which you can consume or store on videotape (for personal use). You can now buy Walkman-style systems for which you needn't purchase tapes, CDs or any physical manifestation, but pay instead for downloading intangible data files (mp3s) from the Internet. Increasingly, what is valued in our culture is not matter but data, not atoms but bits, as explored eloquently in Nicholas Negroponte's book, *Being Digital*.

This non-materialism leads us to a new kind of

secularism. Christians have spent a lot of the twentieth century arguing with materialists that there is more to the universe than what can be seen and touched. The new atheists have no problem with that; in fact, their world-view is likely to look down upon the material universe. The characters of William Gibson's epoch-making novel *Neuromancer* refer to their bodies in a derogatory way as 'the meat'. And *Jargon Watch*, a dictionary of the digital revolution, lists the word 'meat-space' for the physical world as opposed to the virtual. Increasingly, our dialogue is with people caught up not in materialism but in a new Platonism – a techno-gnosticism, in which knowledge is what's most important and physical reality is regarded as a barrier to communication and information. The Christian gospel must be communicated in a very different way to people of so different a mind-set.

The role of Christians

What then is our role as Christians in a society contemplating wide-scale adoption of computer (or other) technologies? One thing we will almost certainly be unable to accomplish is to save any of our sandcastles by fighting those waves.

Probably the most important thing for Christians to do is to *be Christian* in everything that we do. We are not to be conformed to this world (Rom 12:2); rather, we were told by Jesus to be in the world but not of it (John 17). We are not to withdraw from society – we will probably use computers in the same way that we use telephones and cars. But even if these technologies have the power to change what our society says and believes, they won't change what *we* say and believe. We are in the society, speaking *to* the society, but are not *of* the society. Being a Christian means constantly seeing the things (and non-things) of this world in the light of creation, in the light of eternity, in the light of the cross.

Specifically, then, we Christians should be thinking through our evangelistic strategy. If I am right and we are moving away from materialism, then what is it that we will be prophetically saying to our culture and to the people around us? We may, ironically, find ourselves in the position of having to *affirm* physical reality and the human side of the incarnation rather than just spiritual reality.

In connection with that, in the twenty-first century, Christians should be known as people who value face-to-face, live communication across a diversity of groups. A congregation of mixed races, ages and styles worshipping together and enjoying each other will be an astonishing witness to the average twenty-first century person.

Let's get out into the water! We cannot, perhaps, fight to hold back the tide, but enough people standing firm can form a wave-break to moderate the effects of the waves. Others will be called and gifted to surf, mapping the flow with their progress.

Even if robots do not take over our lives, computer technology will certainly mould the society in which we live. Technology must be viewed as a tool or medium through which we express our Christian-ness – in the world but not of the world, in cyberspace but not of cyberspace. We must not be conformed to this or any other temporary world, for our address is, ultimately, in a 'domain' or world that is more alive, more solid, more real.

Chapter 9

The challenge of pluralism: Truth and reality in a postmodern culture

Peter Hicks

The apostle Paul
Castle Jail, Caesarea.

Dear Paul,
  Help!
  I'm a Christian living in the twenty-first century, and I've got a problem.
  Briefly, it's this. I want to persuade people that Christianity is true, just like you did in the first century. But people nowadays don't believe in truth like they used to – it's all subjective and relative. I tried it with a friend yesterday – told her all about Jesus and the fact that he really lived and taught all sorts of fantastic things, and died, and rose again – just the sort of thing you'd do. And she listened and took it all in, and said it was very interesting.
  So I said, 'It's not just interesting; it's true. And if it's true, then surely you must do something about it.'
  She said, 'Ah, that depends on what you mean by "true". As far as I'm concerned, there's no such thing as fixed and final truth in the old-fashioned sense. For me, truth is relative. It's what any individual makes it. We

each decide what is true for us. Christianity may be true for you, but that doesn't make it true for me.'

'But it's in the Bible,' I said. 'Don't you accept the authority of the Bible?'

She just laughed. 'Of course not. I don't accept any authority.'

That led us off at a tangent. I tried to show her that it was impossible to live without at least some kind of authority. She may reject the authority of the Bible, but she had to accept the authority of, say, gravity, which stopped her jumping up to the moon. I think I persuaded her on that one, but she still wouldn't buy the Bible thing.

So what do I do? I guess it was easy for you in the first century – you just had to say, 'The Bible says', and everyone accepted it. But things are different now. Help!

Yours,

Justin.

Justin,
The twenty-first century.

Dear Justin,

You have thoroughly depressed me, on two counts.

First, you're living in the twenty-first century. I couldn't believe it when I read that! Only yesterday I was trying to take my mind off my surroundings (this place stinks!) by trying to work out how long it would be before the Lord Jesus returns, if the church goes on growing at its present rate. I reckoned about fifty years max. And there you are, two thousand years down the line, and the job's still not done! What on earth's gone wrong?

But the second depressing thing is your bit about it being easy for me in the first century. I don't know where you got that from! What makes you think I go around expecting people to accept the authority of the Bible? Why should they? They've all got their holy writings they choose to believe in. It's only the Jews who accept the authority of the Bible, and there's so much prejudice against us Jews that just referring to the Jewish writings is enough to put many people off completely.

Of course, when I'm talking to Jews, I do appeal to the authority of the Bible. And if I find a non-Jew who for some reason is able to accept it, then fine. But for most people, you have to start where they're at. If they're into mystery religions – you know, sort of New Agey stuff – you have to use the language of the mystery religions. Or if they're into Greek poets and philosophers, you have to start with those.

'Truth is relative,' says your friend, as though that's something new. Well, there's nothing new under the sun. You can't have a more relativistic age than the first century. The place is awash with a huge range of religions and philosophies. You pays your money and you takes your choice. And why should that surprise us? If they haven't got the one Creator God as the basis of truth and meaning and everything else, of course they'll end up in relativism. Haven't you read the story of the tower of Babel?

So where's your problem?

Grace and peace,

Paul.

The apostle Paul,
Castle Jail, Caesarea.

Dear Paul,

Sorry.

I didn't mean to depress you. And I admit I didn't know that you lived in a culture that was just as relativistic as the twenty-first century. But when I started thinking about it, I realised that this was bound to be so. I've done a bit of study on the development of Western philosophy, and I know that it was Christianity that provided the basis for everything that's significant in Western thought and Western culture – things like meaning and purpose, truth and goodness, right and wrong, and so on. It's because our culture has abandoned the Christian world-view as its basis that we have now collapsed into relativism. Of course, the first century – before Christianity had begun to mould the culture – was just at the place where we've arrived nearly two thousand years later.

I'm sorry if this depresses you further, but at least you're in a strong position to give me some ideas as to what I might do.

Yours,

Justin.

Justin,
The twenty-first century.

Dear Justin,

After I sent off my reply to your first letter I felt really bad that I'd been so tough with you. I'm afraid I do get very depressed in this prison: I'm in solitary at the moment – a tiny cell right under the castle with hardly any light; the only running water is what seeps through the walls. And it stinks. It's not so bad when I'm in the common jail – at least there's company and I can tell the prisoners about Jesus. A captive audience, you might say.

But listen. You talk about relativism as though it's some great curse – a major problem that makes preaching the gospel much harder. Why should it be so? Preaching the gospel is always hard (how many years have you spent in prison?). But why should we assume it's harder to preach in a relativistic age than in an indifferent age or a violently antagonistic age? In some ways I think it's easier when the world-view of the people you're talking to is very different from that of Jesus. There's a lot to be said for being able to present a radically different alternative.

So you want advice? Well, I've already told you the vital first step you need to take – start where these people are at. Get into their mind-set. Why do they think the way they think? What about, in your next letter, listing some of the people you know, and analysing why they think what they think? That would help me with giving advice, but it would also start you on the road of getting inside their skins, so that you can really begin to communicate with them.

Grace and peace,

Paul.

The apostle Paul,
Castle Jail, Caesarea.

Dear Paul,

OK, here goes.

Chloe says she doesn't believe anything. There are no such things as truth or goodness or the like. She says all the people she's ever met are just out for themselves, and they all say or do whatever will bring them out on top. Everything's a kind of power struggle: nothing's real, nothing's fixed; it's all just a kind of meaningless mess.

And my analysis? She's been incredibly hurt. Her parents broke up when she was a kid. All her life people have let her down, told her lies, broken their promises. She's had a rotten deal from life, so she can't trust anybody, can't believe anything.

Then there's Sam – he's the opposite. Secure home, well-off, nice family, good job. But no interest in God. Science explains everything. No need for anything else.

And Mike. Out for kicks – anything that kicks. Sex, drugs, football, raves, punch-ups. Why? I guess because he's bored – totally, killingly bored.

Then there's Karen. Career girl. Focussed – wow, is she focussed! Nothing else matters; she's going to get to the top. She'll do anything to get there. Why? I guess it's because she needs to prove herself – to arrive, be recognised, own a Porsche. Why? Because that's what counts in our society. You don't matter unless you're on top.

Is that enough? What would you do with that lot?

Yours,

Justin.

Justin,
The twenty-first century.

Dear Justin,

Hey, what interesting friends you have. I'd really enjoy meeting them. Hurt. No needs. Bored. And out to prove herself.

What would I do with that lot?

I'd give them something big. Something fantastically bigger than their narrow little world-view.

'No such things as truth or goodness.'

'Science explains everything.'

'Totally, killingly bored.'

'A Porsche is to arrive.'

They're like people scratching around for the scraps thrown to the dogs when there's an incredible feast spread for them.

I'd show them something real, that's got all the things Chloe doesn't believe in, that's bigger than science, that kicks far better than drugs and makes a Porsche look like a baby's rattle.

That's what they need. Show them the feast. Let them know what they're missing.

Grace and peace,

Paul.

The apostle Paul,
Castle Jail, Caesarea.

Paul,
    You are frustrating!
    'Something big,' you say. 'Something real.'
    What? And how?
    Yours,
    Justin.

Justin,
The twenty-first century.

Dear Justin,
    Jesus – or, to put it another way, the Lord of Glory. The Christ. The Alpha and Omega. God over all. Your Lord and ours. The Name that is above every name. The fullness of God. The Judge of the living and the dead. The Coming One, and tons more.
    I thought it was obvious. You can't get bigger than that. All those other ways of living and viewing the world are shadows – they look real when they're all you can see, when you're in the darkness. But bring in a bit of light, and you'll soon show up their emptiness.
    How? Every way. But especially in you. And in other Christians. Chloe rejects reality and truth, goodness and meaning. You won't get far arguing with her. But show her something that's real – goodness that is palpable, truth that is powerful, meaning that really works. Show her Jesus, the way, the truth, the life. Even more signifi-

cantly, show her Jesus the one she really can trust, who gives her unconditional love, who has what it takes to heal all her hurt.

And Sam. He doesn't really need arguments either, though you could try to show him that even on his presuppositions there's got to be something, or someone, behind the whole scientific show. What will change him is meeting a real person, the living Christ, something much more interesting than a scientific machine...

Mike's a tough one. We've got plenty of Mikes around here. Most of them are simply selfish – just out for what they can get for themselves. So it won't really work to tell them that Jesus is going to provide their next kick – that'll only play to their selfishness. We've got to offer them something stronger. We've got to show them Jesus as the radical alternative to kicks. You've got to stretch Mike's horizons so that he can see something so big that it shows up the incredible pettiness of all the things he's into at the moment.

And Karen? She's going for the big time because she thinks that's the greatest. You and I know that Jesus is the greatest. So she needs to meet Jesus.

Simple, isn't it?

Grace and peace,

Paul.

The apostle Paul,
Castle Jail, Caesarea.

Dear Paul,
   No, it isn't.
   You make it sound as if all I have to do is tell them
about Jesus.
   But they don't want to know about Jesus.
   Yours,
   Justin.

Justin,
The twenty-first century.

Dear Justin,
   I didn't say anything about telling them about Jesus. I
talked about their meeting Jesus, and you showing them
Jesus.
   I accept there is a place for talking about Jesus – I do
it whenever I can. But I never do it on its own, and sometimes I deliberately don't do it until the person I'm with
is ready to hear it. I don't waste pearls on pigs.
   What these people need is Jesus, not talk about him.
Reality, not arguments; the demonstration of the Spirit's
power, not wise and persuasive words. Then, when they
fall down in front of you and say, 'What must I do to be
saved?', you can tell them.
   Grace and peace,
   Paul.

The apostle Paul,
Castle Jail, Caesarea.

Dear Paul,

I can see where you're going.

You're saying that Chloe and Sam and co won't buy into the Christian world-view, but if they see the real thing – Jesus himself, fantastically real and alive in my life – that'll make them realise there is something in Christianity, and then I'll be able to tell them what it is.

But this is making one big assumption – that my life is so full of Jesus and his truth and goodness, they can actually see it.

And the fact is, it isn't.

That's the difference between you and most Christians today. You wrote all those amazing things like 'Christ lives in me', 'to live is Christ', 'Christ in you', and God spreading everywhere through you 'the fragrance of the knowledge of Christ'. But most Christians today are no different from anybody else. We don't live Jesus any more.

I guess that's why we feel so helpless.

Sorry if this depresses you.

Yours,

Justin.

Justin,
The twenty-first century.

Dear Justin,

No, it doesn't depress me. To tell you the truth, it's nothing new. There are people around here who claim to be Christians but who live like pagans. And the pagans see them and laugh at their so-called Christianity.

But it doesn't have to be that way. If you're a Christian, you've got Christ in you, and in Christ is all the fullness of God. He is truth and goodness, love, and meaning, and all the rest of it. And he's alive!

Listen. Is there any difference between a seed, say a grain of mustard, and a bit of grit the same size and shape? Of course there is. You put a bit of grit in the ground and nothing happens. Put a seed in the ground and you get a plant. Because there's life in the seed. You or I on our own are like the bit of grit. We start with nothing and we get nothing. But the life of Christ in me produces life in others. It's not me, it's Christ in me. It's not words, it's the power of God. Words on their own won't do it. It's the Spirit who gives life.

Why can't that be true of you?

Grace and peace,

Paul.

The apostle Paul,
Castle Jail, Caesarea.

Dear Paul,

You'll not believe this, but I've never sown a seed in my life.

I think I get what you're saying. In a postmodern age, when people won't accept absolutes or authority or arguments, we have got to get back to the real thing – to a person, a life, the power and presence of God – to Jesus. And, since that's something alive, it's not up to us to make it work. It's already got what it takes to do that by itself. What we have got to do is to make sure we're full of Jesus. And if we're full of Jesus, full of God and the Holy Spirit, then he'll do what needs to be done – he'll meet Chloe's needs, blow Sam's mind, sort out Mike.

It all sounds great and I guess it fits. Postmodernism is into persons and relationships and encounters. And image. It's up to us to 'image' the real thing so that they buy into it and get hooked.

I think I'll go for it, with God's help.

Thanks for everything.

Yours,

Justin.

Chapter 10

The challenge of pluralism: The changing face of religion in Britain

Peter Riddell

How would you describe the situation of religious pluralism in Britain today, and what are some of the challenges and opportunities it presents to Christians?

Britain has undergone a social revolution in all sorts of ways over the last two generations. Since the Second World War there has been a steady intake of immigrants, who have brought with them their cultures and faith systems. This, combined with significant changes in communication and technology, has contributed to the development of substantial non-Christian religious communities in Britain. The largest is Muslim (between 1.5 and 2 million); there is also a substantial community of Hindus (just under 1 million); and there are large communities of Buddhists, Sikhs and various other faiths. There is genuine religious pluralism in Britain in that Christianity is no longer alone. Obviously, this raises an important question: how do we adapt our Christian understanding to a new situation where there are other faiths on our doorstep rather than at a distant location overseas? All sorts of challenges emerge, but with built-in opportunities. No longer do we have to go thousands of miles to get into the midst of those other faith communities. This opens up all kinds of possibilities for learning, and for sharing faith.

How have Christians responded to these challenges and opportunities? Do you think that response has been sufficient and appropriate?

There have been different types of response at the level of the local church. For Christian communities in the towns, villages and cities of Britain, probably the most common response has been to close the shutters, and to ignore the presence of other faith communities and carry on as before. Some feel threatened by them and want to build figurative walls between themselves and other faith communities. Another response, which has tended to come from Christian denominational leadership or ecumenical groups, is the development of dialogue policies.

A further type of response is seen primarily among evangelicals. Sometimes they have seen the presence of other faith communities as a great opportunity, and have actively engaged in mission and outreach in many different ways. Without any doubt, the Christian communities in Britain do need to recognise the presence of other faith communities and not see them as a threat. They need to engage with them in various and creative ways, whose appropriateness may be partly judged by the nature of the response given by various faith groups.

Can you give an example of an inappropriate and an appropriate response?

Whether or not something is appropriate depends on the type of faith held by the person with whom you are interacting. I am primarily thinking about Muslims here, of course, because they are the ones that I know the best. But there are different sorts of Muslims. If you meet a radical Muslim (perhaps 15 per cent of Muslims in Britain) you need a certain set of 'tools' to interact with them. You may be a bit more forthright. It may involve debate, and will certainly involve a level of assertiveness from the Christian side, which you wouldn't want to use with a different sort of Muslim. On the other hand, I know some Muslim parents whose children go to school with mine, and they live their lives just like the rest of us. Their prime concern is the family, the education of their children, and so on. They are not really interested in pushing Islam in a fundamentalist sort of way. The worst thing I could do would be to challenge them in a polemical or confrontational way about their faith, because it would only close doors. What is important is that Christians know with whom they are interacting, and choose appropriate methods for sharing their faith with those particular people.

Why do you think Christians respond in such different ways, from putting up walls to engaging in dialogue?

I think the reasons for the different responses are education and awareness. The response of putting up walls, and wanting to keep the other faith communities at arm's length, grows out of a lack of knowledge about them. Such people tend to see members of the other faith communities not so much as human beings but as representatives of a system. So when such Christians see Muslims, they think of international Islam and the media images of terrorism. They keep as far away from them as possible, rather than seeing them as human beings with the same concerns and, very often, the same interests and the same worries as we have. The response of building dialogue or interacting in different ways with Muslims arises out of awareness, out of knowing the different types of Muslims with whom we are dealing, and realising that we do need to interact with members of other faith communities.

Could you make some suggestions as to how people might respond to Muslims they encounter in the workplace, for example?

I think if there is a standard first response to meeting Muslims in the workplace it is merely to see them as work colleagues first, rather than seeing them as Muslims only: in other words, make friends with them as you would with any other work colleague. Don't define that person by their faith, or by your perception of their faith; see him or her as a human being with a spouse, children, whatever, and make friends. Through the process of friendship, issues of faith will arise, and it is at that point that faith identity naturally enters into the relationship. Then you will have to decide how you are going to react to this person as you respond to his or her faith.

The basic rule is, when you meet people of another faith, although their faith may be central to their identity, you need to see them first as people and not as representatives of a system.

The situation seems a bit more complex when there is a mosque being built round the corner from the local church. Perhaps people in this situation are unable to see the Muslims they are encountering as individuals and friends. How do you think Christians ought to respond to a mosque being built in their neighbourhood?

This is a difficult one, because it has to do with the identity of the neighbourhood. Whether we are talking about the construction of a mosque, or the construction of a big church of a denomination other than our own, or the construction of some landmark which is going to change the existing identity of the community, it is a fact that people feel threatened. A mosque is no different in that way from any other type of new building that can be built, so I think it is natural for Christians to feel some sort of threat. But, at the same time, society does change – society is an evolving thing. Neighbourhoods change in their make-up, and there is nothing we can do about that. We cannot accept the establishment of a system which says that only one type of British citizen will live in a particular neighbourhood and a different type of British citizen will not. There is going to be a movement of populations, and people want to bring the symbols of their faith with them. So, if Muslims move in increasing numbers to a particular neighbourhood, they will want to put up a mosque.

What I am really saying is, I can understand why Christians feel threatened, but I think that they need to adjust to the reality of a new situation. I am a strong believer in freedom of religion, and so I believe that adherents of different faiths have the right to set up their own places of worship. Mosques *are* being built and they are being built in increasing numbers. The fact is, Britain is a multi-religious community, so the authorities need to ensure that a system of unconscious apartheid does not develop. Towns should not become largely Muslim towns or largely Christian towns. Interaction is important because the faith communities do need to mix together. This is how bridges of understanding are built.

How should local churches work with Muslims and other faith groups? Should they make overtures to such faith communities, or should they just quietly coexist?

I think they *should* make overtures, and plenty of churches do so. There are reports of churches making overtures to mosques or Islamic centres which lead to substantial contact between the two communities. Such contact should be the result of a conscious effort. Christians should approach new mosques or Islamic centres, and vice versa – it shouldn't be one-way contact only. If you work next to people and live next to people, you should make friends with them. We should work actively on building those bridges.

Considering the pluralistic nature of British society today, is there room still to make claims for Christian truth? How do we uphold truth claims as Christian when we are interacting with people of other faiths?

That is an important question. I think that recognising the presence of other faith communities, showing respect for them and discussing theology with them, does not imply that we have to compromise the fundamental tenets of our faith. While there are many points of similarity across different faiths, there are some basic points of dissimilarity which we cannot compromise. For example, Muslims are taught that Jesus was not crucified; he did not die and, therefore, he did not rise to life again. Christians can't compromise their doctrine of the death and resurrection of Christ. We can still interact with Muslims and allow for a difference of perspective, but it doesn't mean we have to give up on the basic doctrines of our faith. There is still plenty of room for Christians to hold to the central truths of their faith and to share them with Muslims, and to allow the Muslims to share some central tenets of their faith – provided we are prepared to accept the idea that there are some things we will not be able to agree on. At the end of the day, those who are listening to a partner in dialogue will have to make a decision as to whether they find the explanation of that partner more attractive than the position of their own faith.

Do you think there is still an evangelistic mission to people of other faiths in today's pluralistic society, or is it a matter of sharing some similarities and differences of belief and leaving it at that?

I see evangelistic mission in very broad terms. I see part of the evangelistic mission as the type of dialogue we have just been discussing – sitting down and talking with Muslims or Hindus about what we believe. But another part of mission is saying to the other, 'I believe that this is God-given truth and this is something that you need to consider.' I don't have any problem with doing that, provided *everybody* is allowed to do it. I am a strong supporter of dialogue, but I interpret dialogue very broadly. It includes polite discussions about easy matters, and more robust debates. In any case, dialogue requires true honesty. If the Christian faith calls on us to share what we believe and to invite others to Christ, then being faithful to that should contribute to the dialogue.

How do you think Christians can best deal with any fear or lack of confidence that they might have when they are living in an environment where humanism and other faiths are more prevalent than their own?

To begin with, we need to recognise that different people have different gifts and not everybody should feel pressured to be a street evangelist. I don't think that all Christians should feel that they have to go out and engage with every Muslim they meet and say, 'You need to come to faith in Christ.' What each Christian should do is become more aware: study about the other faiths; learn more about their own faith so that they feel confident in their knowledge of Christianity; and use their gifts appropriately to do what God has gifted them to do. One reason for the lack of confidence among Christians is a lack of knowledge about their own faith. As I am always encouraging Christians to learn about other faiths, I think it is equally essential that Christians should learn more about their own faith – through distance learning programmes if they can't come to full-time study at theological college.

It is important, before Christians take part in dialogue, that they educate themselves: they need to learn about the faith of those with whom they are dialoguing, but they also need to be very clear in their own minds *why* they are engaging in dialogue. I believe there are four striking reasons.

The first one would be to *understand the person with whom you are in dialogue*, to learn more about your neighbour or a neighbouring community, whether Muslim or Buddhist. The second reason is that dialogue can lead to *a clearer understanding of God* because, for us to take part in dialogue, we have to articulate our own faith position. When you have to articulate something, it encourages clarity in your own mind and helps you crystallise your own thoughts. Dialogue pushes us to understand clearly some of the areas of our own faith which we have found difficult or have not really thought about. Third, dialogue provides an opportunity for *witnessing*. If Christians and Muslims come together in a dialogue situation, it offers a perfect opportunity to share our faith and to allow the others to share their faith, too. Fourth, dialogue provides an opportunity for *cooperation* in all sorts of practical areas. Through dialogue, Christians and Muslims in a particular neighbourhood might be able to cooperate to eliminate prostitution in the neighbourhood, or to address various civic services which are lacking, or to talk about media bias against religion.

I think any of those purposes are valid reasons for dialogue. But, before they go into it, Christians need to think about why they are doing it – whether for one of these four purposes, or for other reasons.

How do you see the future of multi-faith Britain?

Of course, the future is a very big thing! Speaking of the short-term future, I think multi-faith Britain will see a number of changes around the edges, but the big picture probably won't change that much. In fifty years' time, Britain will still be a majority Christian country, in terms of a very broad definition of Christianity. I think the minority faith communities will grow somewhat, and the Islamic community will grow but it won't become a majority faith. Where the biggest change may happen is not so much in terms of the movement to Islam in this country, but the movement to Buddhism. Many Christians don't realise that, while we often hear stories about Christians converting to Islam, for every one Christian who is converted to Islam, ten Christians convert to Buddhism. It has a sort of New Age appeal in a pluralistic culture. I think Buddhism will rise significantly in its proportion of faith adherence in this country. But overall, Britain will remain a Christian country in terms of the majority.

*Some say one of the attractions of Buddhism is its inclusivist
nature. Could you describe the difference between inclusivist
and exclusivist religions?*

In terms of historical Christianity, a strongly exclusivist
approach understands Christ as providing the only path
to salvation and access to divine truth: in other words, all
other religions are wrong and excluded from the truth.
Inclusivism means that, in terms of the Christian paradigm, salvation may be found through Christ but there
are elements of truth in other faiths, and you can take
them and build on them by adding Christ. At its
extreme, exclusivism tends to demolish other faiths,
while inclusivism affirms them.

*Do you think the desire that some Christians have for a more
inclusivist faith is a result of the pluralism – and relativism – in
our postmodern society?*

Unquestionably. It is easy to be exclusivist when you
don't see the human face of the other. When Muslims
were thousands of miles away, they were more a concept
than a neighbour. It was much easier to be an exclusivist
and to say, 'We have the only true religion.'

In a more pluralist society, Christians could see that
many others also were earnestly seeking God. One thing
we share with Muslims is a desire for God. We may not
agree on how to find God, but we are certainly
searching for the same thing. We happen to be driven
by the same desire to find and please God. When some
Christians saw that aspect of other faiths, inclusivism
naturally resulted and became the dominant attitude

towards other religions in many churches.

What does it say about the integrity of any religion if we suggest that they are all the same, equally true and equally valid? Should Christianity be an inclusivist faith or resist inclusivism?

Well, that would depend on your understanding of 'inclusivism'. As I would be comfortable using the term, it would mean that we recognise in Islam some truths and elements of beauty. But to uphold the integrity of Christianity, we would have to say that Islam is incomplete: Islam needs Christ and the redemption that Christ offers. This would involve not only completion but some doctrinal reformation of Islam. There is much within the Islamic scriptures, and some of the great Islamic writers, that we share. But it needs something more – Christ and the redemption he offers. This kind of inclusivism has a certain appeal.

Should Christians pray with people from other faiths? I am thinking especially in terms of some sort of public meeting where people representing a variety of faiths are invited to participate.

This is an important question and something I feel very strongly about. I totally support prayer with others on condition – and only on condition – that it is honest prayer: in other words, that Christians pray as they would normally pray, allowing the others to pray as they would normally pray. When we enter into dialogue, or participate in joint worship services, we should be honest to our faith. We shouldn't wear masks and only pray in a way that we think will please the other. We have got to pray the way we would normally pray as Christians. So, if we pray through Christ to God, then that is what we should be doing when we are praying in front of a Muslim, not doing it differently because a Muslim is present. If we have to water it down, then no, I wouldn't pray.

The world is a much smaller place than it used to be. Do these issues raise any concerns beyond our own borders?

An issue that is raised often by Christians and Muslims is the treatment of religious minorities in this country compared to the treatment of Christian minorities in other countries. I am a strong believer in reciprocity. I fully support religious minority rights in this country, so that Muslims, for example, are free to build their own mosques, to practise their faith and to share their faith. I fully support that. But I think it is fair to expect that Christian minorities in Muslim locations should be free to do the same thing, and sadly this is often not the case. In some Muslim countries, the practice of any faith other than Islam is banned. There are no churches and, from time to time, foreign workers who are Christians are arrested for holding clandestine Christian worship services. In many Muslim locations, Christian communities are unable to get government approval to repair churches because there is official obstruction to the practice of other faiths. I think we need to recognise the importance of the work that the World Evangelical Fellowship is doing through its Religious Liberty Commission in demanding that Christian minorities in non-Christian countries have the same rights of freedom of worship and freedom to share their faith as do Muslim minorities or other faith minorities in many Christian countries. I think this is a very important thing to push for, and it should be explored further by our religious authorities in the West.

How can Christians remain positive, rather than negative, about this issue? It is easy to suggest that if Christians don't have freedom elsewhere, then various religions ought not to have freedom here.

Sometimes you hear this Christian response. Some hear the negative stories reported in the media about Christians being persecuted in a village somewhere on the other side of the world, so they draw the line here by saying no to building a mosque down the road in a British town. I think the best approach is to bring up the issue of reciprocity during dialogue session with Muslims in Britain, for example. If Christians have heard of a particular Christian community under pressure from Muslim authorities, they can seek the support of local Muslim authorities in this country through statements of solidarity with the Christian community. There have been several incidents where this has happened very constructively. In February 1997, a Christian village in Pakistan was destroyed by a mob from a Muslim community, and the villagers were cast out of their homes. There were strong statements of support from Christians here in Britain, but a number of Muslim leaders here also offered statements of sympathy for what had happened to the Christian community. It led to a visit to that community by British church leaders accompanied by several Muslim leaders from the British Muslim community. In another case in Pakistan, during the Afghanistan crisis in October 2001, Muslim extremists shot and killed seventeen Christians during Sunday worship. The Muslim Council of Britain was very quick to denounce the attacks, offering expressions of sympathy to the families of the victims. This is very encouraging in terms of dialogue and cooperation, but it also highlights the issue of reciprocity. I think this is what we have got to be seeking: Christians and Muslims extending the same hand of hospitality to religious minorities in their majority countries as they demand elsewhere.

You mention the Afghanistan crisis. What effect is that having on the relationship between Christians and Muslims in Britain?

The Afghanistan crisis is, of course, part of a bigger set of events, brought to the fore by the terrorist attacks on the World Trade Center and the Pentagon on 11 September, 2001.

As far as the impact on relations between Christians and Muslims in this country is concerned, we need to be careful not to speak in terms of a fundamental opposition of the two groups. When the terrorist attacks occurred on September 11 there were expressions of horror from both Christians and Muslims in Britain. Many Muslims were as forthright in condemning the attacks as were Christians. So you could argue that events such as 11 September have actually cemented relationships between many Christians and Muslims in this country as they saw eye to eye on the awfulness of what happened.

When Prime Minister Tony Blair stressed that the conflict was between the West and Islam on the one side, and terrorism on the other, I think he was quite right. Here in Britain Christians and Muslims are united in condemning terror. Support for the terrorist attacks, for the Taliban, and for Osama Bin Laden and others, comes from some Muslims, but they are not representative of the British Muslim community as a whole.

So the crisis has not driven a wedge between Christians and Muslims in this country. But it has clearly highlighted the need to deal with the threat posed by Islamic radicalism, a threat which is felt by Christians and by the majority of Muslims, who are fair-minded, sensible and balanced. On that matter we can agree, and work together for the good of the whole community, as one in which people may live and worship in freedom.

Chapter 11

Taking up the challenge: Being church in today's world

Jane Rennie

> I am often struck by the church notice-board slogan which reads, 'Christ is the answer'. I suspect that many would be prompted to respond, 'Yes, but does the church know what the question is?'
>
> *(Laurie Green, Let's Do Theology, Mowbray, 1998, p1)*

As I look at today's world, I have no doubts that the church notice-board slogan is true. I have seen in my own life, and in the lives of many others, the evidence for this assertion. As a Christian, I seek to 'live by faith, not by sight' (2 Cor 5:7) and so I stand in the eternal truth that Christ *is* the answer and *will be* the answer. For me, the standpoint of faith is not to live in denial or unreality, but to have confidence in God and the truth of his Word.

However, I have sympathy with Green's response. Does the church understand the questions the world is asking? Are we even listening? Perhaps we are overwhelmed by the complexities of life today. Perhaps we doubt whether we can answer the world's questions. And yet we do have the answer – we have Christ. The issue for the church is how to express that answer, how to make Christ known.

For me, this is the key challenge for the church today: how to hear the world's questions and make Christ, The Answer – *their* answer – known. That challenge has little to do with how I should cope with living in the world. To be honest, I am happy to be 'an alien and stranger in the world' (1 Pet 2:11), but this does not mean that I wish to retreat from the world, or think that the church should retreat from the world: rather, it means a shift in focus – a shift from me, from us, from the church, to *them*.

As young Christian leaders, my husband and I sought to run church, good church – sound, friendly and entertaining. We educated, cared for and served the flock. As I look back to that first church now, I often think not of the people who were in it but of the people who were outside of it. What did we do for *them*? What *were* we to them? Do they remember us as those who made Christ known to them? My focus is now unashamedly evangelistic. I am ready to admit to a certain bias in this respect. However, as I look at the church growth statistics, and particularly the level of conversion growth, my conclusion is that this bias is justified. My passion is now for the lost, for those who do not know that Christ is the answer.

Robert Warren highlights the need for the church to move from 'pastoral mode' to 'mission mode':

> The church in 'pastoral mode' is a church in Christendom setting....The church in 'mission mode' is, in contrast, set in a culture where a number of competing value systems and world-views exist alongside each other. Such is the present setting of the church. This is why we need a missionary church.
>
> (*Robert Warren, Building Missionary Congregations, Church House Publishing, 1995, p3*)

Born in the sixties and shaped by the eighties, I could tend quite happily towards an individualistic orientation to my faith and mission as a Christian. Yet I am convinced that to see the type of church growth and levels of conversion we desire to see in Britain, and in the world, will take a corporate effort. Modern management theory teaches us that the key to competitive advantage is the mobilisation of every ounce of intelligence and energy in our organisations, drawing out the best from the *whole* workforce and not just the few.[1] True for the marketplace, it is also true for the church – we need everyone to be involved (Luke 10:2). Therefore, as I consider today's world I cannot consider it as an isolated individual. My response to the world must be corporate: the *church* must present the answer; the *church* must make Christ known.

Being church

How can the church make Christ known? What is the appropriate method in today's world? As John Habgood asks, 'Given the present state of society in Britain today what ought the churches be trying to do?'

One way to address this issue is to look at it stylistically. What style of church, what types of music, what variety of lighting effects do we need?[2] However, for me, that is not the heart of the issue. We can change the inside of the church as much as we like but, as the world rarely enters the church, we may find this strategy less effective than we had hoped. The question is more one of 'being', of what we are as a church. Charles Green outlined four aspects of 'being church' –· pastoral, priestly, prophetic and evangelistic.[3] I will use these four headings as a framework for an analysis of how the church can begin to make Christ known in today's world.

Being a pastoral church

The church I belong to seeks to identify itself as a non-pastoral congregation. When we express our identity in this way, panic can often result: 'Not pastoral? You must be pastoral! People need pastoring' Actually, we are an extremely pastoral church, but we have sought to re-draw the pastoral boundaries or, I would argue, to draw them as they were originally intended. In Luke 15, Jesus tells the parable of the lost sheep for whom the shepherd leaves the ninety-nine sheep to go and find. As we seek as a church to make Christ known to today's world, I believe we need to take up the pastoral commission to pastor the one-hundredth sheep. Ed Silvoso writes:

> The Bible tells us that the shepherd leaves the 99 sheep alone, safely tucked away in the fold, in order to go after the lost one. He actually makes the one-hundredth sheep the focus of his care and attention.
>
> (*Ed Silvoso*, That None should Perish, *Regal, 1994, p84*)

How can we do this? One way is to identify social needs and seek to meet them. The church has actually done this successfully for many years, running mothers and toddlers groups, debt-counselling services, support for the elderly, and so on. These methods can be and are effective, but perhaps in today's world we need to approach the issue from a slightly different perspective.

One facet of today's postmodern world is the emphasis on relationships. The 'social service' model the church has used to pastor people can often seem non-relational. Structured, impersonal, meeting people's perceived needs, it can often ignore their 'felt', experienced needs. Therefore, as we seek to be a pastoral church, we need to bring our pastoring down to the relational, personal level. We need to move away from the institutional, and get individual Christians involved in the lives of individual non-Christians. Christ is the answer not just for your neighbour in the pew, but also for your neighbour in your street and your neighbour at work. As Roger Forster has expressed it, we need 'the sacrifice on the ground of loving our neighbours, the people around us, and bringing them into touch with Jesus'.[4] And Stanley Grenz: 'Our gospel must address the human person within the context of the communities in which people are embedded.'[5]

David is a man in his thirties. His community is his local pub. In the last six months, David has met a Christian who has also made the pub his community. David has shared with this Christian the relationship problems he is having. He has talked about his life and God's place in it. He has been prayed for in the pub, in front of friends. Interestingly, his friends were keen to join in the prayer, showing perhaps that those outside the church can often display more faith in God than those inside. David sang carols in the pub this Christmas as church came to the pub. David is finding Jesus outside of the church institution. He is becoming part of the church and all without stepping inside the church.

Being a priestly church

Coming from the nonconformist tradition, I was always

keen to assert the importance of the priesthood of all believers (1 Pet 2:5–9). I understood this as an expression of my right to come before God on my own, without an earthly mediator. I could come to God solely through Jesus (Heb 4:14–16). My conception of priesthood was totally individualistic. The paradigm shift I needed to make here, and which I believe the church needs to make, is to see the *community* aspect of our priesthood. Priesthood has always been about the community: we are priests not just for ourselves but for our world.[6] So

Priesthood has always been about the community: we are priests not just for ourselves but for our world.

what does it mean to be a priest for the world? In Hebrews, we read that the priest is called to represent humanity in matters related to God (Heb 5:1), and he is to be a mediator between humanity and God, as Jesus is (Heb 7:25; Rom 8:34).

In a study guide relating to the area of Christian living in the workplace, the following statement appeared: 'Before you talk to John about God, first talk to God about John.'[7] This comment draws me back to the subject of mediation. Perhaps, the authors' intention was to encourage their readers to speak to God about John in terms of asking for boldness in talking to John about God. This is a perfectly acceptable and biblical thing to do (Acts 4:29). However, I think an alternative approach is to see it as interceding for John, representing him to God, telling God about him, and asking for God's mercy and blessing to be extended to him.

In Ezekiel 22, we see God looking for a person to 'stand in the gap' – someone who would stand before God on behalf of the land so that God would not destroy it. Dutch Sheets uses this passage from Ezekiel to establish the role of intercession in the church. Sheets presents intercession not just as an option but as an awesome responsibility. He sees God saying the following through Ezekiel:

> 'While my justice demanded judgement, My love wanted forgiveness. Had I been able to find a human to ask Me to spare this people, I could have. It would have allowed Me to show mercy. Because I found no one, however, I had to destroy them.'
>
> (Dutch Sheets, *Intercessory Prayer*, Regal, 1996, p32)

The Bible states quite clearly that we should pray and intercede for our world, 'for everyone – for kings and all those in authority' (1 Tim 2:1). Being church in today's world includes 'standing in the gap' on the world's behalf. Being church in today's postmodern, relational, community-orientated world means doing this not just at the global and national level but at the local level – 'standing in the gap' for your neighbour and your community.

Ed Silvoso has been an important promoter of a concept called 'lighthouses of prayer'.[8] A simple idea, it basically involves you 'standing in the gap' for a particular piece of land and its people. Generally speaking, the land is your neighbourhood – the land and the people in the twenty homes that surround your home. The land, however, could be your workplace, the office you work in and the adjacent offices, your class at school, your hall of residence at college. Establishing a lighthouse of prayer involves your committing to pray for the people around you, weekly, daily if possible – to be their representative before God so that his mercy might be made known to them.

Being a prophetic church

Paul encourages us to eagerly desire spiritual gifts, especially the gift of prophecy, because 'everyone who prophesies speaks to men for their strengthening, encouragement and comfort' (1 Cor 14:1–3). It is sometimes hard to tie this picture of prophecy up with the words of the prophets we find in the Old Testament. There the prophets often spoke to those outside of Israel, who were not numbered among God's people. They spoke to cities, nations and individuals.[9] Often the words they spoke did not seem to carry with them a strong sense of strengthening, encouraging or comforting. So, if the church is to be prophetic, I believe we need to be asking questions about the nature of its prophetic ministry. First, we need to ask where the prophetic ministry of the church should be exercised; and, second, we need to ask what the purpose of the prophetic ministry of the church should be.

The message is not the problem. Christ is the answer but we, the church, are not speaking – or are not speaking in a way that can be heard.

For most of us, prophecy currently happens inside the church: it is about us corporately as a body of God's people and, more commonly, it is about me as an individual.[10] Since becoming a Christian, I have been blessed by both of these uses of the prophetic gift, and have exercised the gift myself in both. However, as we look to the church's role in today's world we need, again, to shift our focus. As I have outlined above, the prophets in the Old Testament did not restrict their prophecies to the people of God. He wants to speak to his world. He spoke through Jesus, his final and perfect Word, but that Word must be made known.

We are confronted today by a world with many questions, a world seeking answers. John Drane describes a group of people he calls the 'spiritual searchers', a group he sees as crucial for the mission of the church: 'For them, the main difficulty with the church is just its irrelevance: it has lost the ability to speak to them.'[11] Reading this, one thing is obvious to me: the message is not the problem. Christ is the answer, but we, the church, are not speaking – or are not speaking in a way that can be heard. We need to re-discover our prophetic voice so that we can bring God's words to our world. In 1 Chronicles, we read of the 'men of Issachar, who understood the times and knew what Israel should do' (1 Chron 12:32). I believe we need some men and women of Issachar. The world not only needs them but, in increasingly tumultuous times, wants them desperately. So the answer to my first question, where should the church's prophetic ministry be exercised, is clear: it should be exercised in the world and not just the church. Paul Stevens writes: 'The church is God's greatest prophet/preacher in history.'[12] Roger Forster goes further: 'A church that does not want to be prophetic is not a church at all.'[13]

Stanley Grenz describes today's postmodern world as post-rationalistic.[14] The world today is not going to be satisfied simply with an apparently logical set of doctrines. For years, the church has struggled to present such a faith, because in a modern world we seemed to have no alternative. Now the playing field of culture has changed and we can take advantage of that. We have a supernatural, holistic gospel that can now be communicated openly and completely to a world looking for answers beyond the natural and beyond knowledge: a world looking, as Grenz puts it, for 'wisdom'.[15]

I visited the home of a non-Christian recently. A single mum called Stella, she was becoming frightened by 'ghosts' in her house. A few years ago, I would have spent much of my time seeking to persuade Stella that ghosts do not exist. However, times have changed and I have changed. On this visit, I listened to Stella's fears, and assured her that God was good and loved her and her children. Then my friends and I prayed for Stella. We prayed for her children. And we prayed for the house, room by room. We spoke into Stella's life. We spoke about her involvement with the occult, no longer arguing the existence of the supernatural but, rather, that God was good and Satan was not. That night Stella decided to change the way she lived her life. Stella heard God's words to her about how she lived. She listened and she changed.

In one London borough, the council recently adopted a new mission and values statement. What values did it adopt? On this occasion, God's. Churches in the borough, working together, made representation to the council. They presented a set of godly values and asked the council to adopt them. The council said yes. The council read the values and saw the wisdom of them. Actually, this is not that surprising, because God is wise and his precepts give 'joy to the heart' and 'light to the eyes' (Ps 19:8). So the answer to my second question, what should be the purpose of the church's prophetic ministry, is also clear. The purpose is that men, women and children should hear the voice of God and be given the opportunity to respond to him. Let's start speaking – I believe the world is listening.

Being an evangelistic church

You may have noticed a common theme running through this discussion on 'being' church. Basically, the thrust is that we should be looking outward, not inward. The things we have done for ourselves – pastoring, praying, prophesying – should now be done for others. In fact, they should be done for others *first*.

Another theme running through this discussion is that of 'being'. I am a functional person, good at doing. As a church, I believe we are often much better at 'doing' than 'being'. We 'do' things – missions, events, services, programmes, meetings, the list goes on. Evangelism is something we do. Actually, it is often something we think about doing, talk about doing, feel a great deal of guilt about not doing, but actually seem expert at putting off. How many evangelistic missions have you taken part in, when you managed to avoid telling anyone about Jesus? Personally, I can list quite a few. I served in different ways, cooking, teaching the Christians, pastoring the team – after all, I am not an evangelist. Obviously, I cannot ignore the fact that Paul listed the ministry of evangelist alongside prophets, pastors and teachers (Eph 4:11). However, I do not believe this excuses those of us not called specifically to this ministry from being evangelistic: the great commission does not seem to offer exclusion clauses (Matt 28:19–20).

I recently visited Argentina, which has seen phenomenal church growth in the last few decades. Many would be happy to link the words 'revival' and 'Argentina' together. If you compare the numbers saved there to the numbers saved in our own Welsh and Hebridian revivals, you could not argue with that link being justified. With something of the spirit of Thomas[16] running through my veins, I went to see for myself.

What did I find? I did not find non-Christians falling into the kingdom like ripe apples from a tree – I found a church that was evangelistic. I did not find a church with full-time, paid evangelists – I found ordinary Christians seeking everyday to share Jesus. They shared Jesus with neighbours, family, friends, colleagues and strangers. In Argentina, if you told your pastor you hadn't led anyone to Christ that month, they would be just as concerned about you as if you told them you had not prayed that month. Evangelism is a Christian discipline; it is part of daily discipleship. It is not easy; it is not private; and you don't really get time off. I think of taxi journeys taken with Argentinian Christians. They saw the taxi driver as someone God loved, someone God wanted to know and to save, someone for whom they were responsible and therefore someone to whom they reached out. They would offer prayer to taxi drivers, waitresses and neighbours; they would talk about Jesus and his offer of salvation. I thought of taxi journeys I had taken around London, when I saw the fact that the taxi driver wanted to speak to me as an intrusion on my privacy. If we are functionally evangelistic, we can be off-duty; if we are evangelistic in our being, then that is what we are and will be at all times.

In the light of the decline in the church, the actual amount of conversion happening must be terrifyingly low.

Let me share a statistic with you. If each evangelical Christian in this country converted one person a year, and if each of those converts did the same, allowing for a 50 per cent drop-out rate in those converted, we would see everyone in England saved in ten years. Each

Christian converting just one person a year. I believe that to make disciples is our primary calling as Christians. If this is the case, then one person a year does not seem a very high target. Looking at that statistic, the frightening truth is that, in the light of the decline in the church, the actual amount of conversion happening must be terrifyingly low. I think we are ashamed – ashamed to talk openly about how few people we have led to Christ. I think we have lost hope because we have seen so little, for so long.

Christ is the answer. We have the answer. We need desperately to regain our confidence in the gospel and begin sharing it again (Rom 1:16).

The way ahead

> We have scarcely begun to scratch the surface in discovering what a vibrant community of faith might need to look like if it is to address the needs of post-modern people. It will require a more fundamental overhaul of our own current styles of church than most of us realise, or are ready for.
>
> (John Drane, *The McDonaldization of the Church*, Darton, Longman & Todd, 2000, p7)

Many people are trying to find new ways of 'doing' church: missionary congregations, cell church, purpose-driven church, seeker-friendly, G12 are just some of the ways and means presented to us. I have great sympathy for those developing them, and believe we can learn from them all. However, I do not believe any system will hold the ultimate answer or be the ultimate solution. With a background in the study of organisational behaviour, I would love to see the answer in a system. However, for the church as for the world, Christ is the answer.

If we are to reach our world for Christ, to make him known, and to make disciples of all nations, then the starting point must be a change in attitude, not a change in the system. We must desire to make Jesus known. Our behaviour must become intentionally evangelistic. We must be evangelistic. Once we have turned to face the world, we must listen to it with clarity of mission and purpose. We must hear the people who are 'harassed and helpless' (Matt 9:36), and have compassion on them, pastoring them and meeting their needs. We must 'stand in the gap', the gulf, the chasm, between God and our neighbour, praying for them, bringing them before our God who so longs to be their God also. *We* must speak God's word into the lives of individuals and communities – God does have a message for them.

These are simple things, things done individually and often. But, when all of those who name the name of Christ do them together, then I believe we can see today's world reached for Christ.

> He's taking us to the potter's table
> Throwing us onto the spinning wheel
> Moulding us with strong hands of mercy
> Preparing us for an amazing yield
> It's the only way ... we need a massive change
> It's for the harvest ... that we are turning
> We're turning inside out
> Out into this world.
>
> (*From Godfrey Birtill's CD*, Outrageous Grace, *Whitefield Music 2000; www.godfreyb.com*)

Endnotes

1   This idea has been most clearly expressed by the Japanese industrialist, Konosuke Matsushita.

2   See John Drane, *McDonaldization of the Church: Spirituality, Creativity and the Future of the Church*, Darton, Longman & Todd, 2000, for a good discussion of how to change the style of church.

3   Charles Green, writing as Chair of the Industrial and Economic Affairs Committee of the Church of England's Board of Social Responsibility, in a booklet entitled *Church and Economy*, 1989.

4   Roger Forster speaking at the Baptist's Mainstream Conference in Swanwick 2001. The conference also included a session on town eldership by the Rev Peter Nodding, who spoke about needing ministries that were 'community minded, not only church minded'.

5   Stanley Grenz, *A Primer on Postmodernism*, Eerdmans, 1996, p169.

6   See R Paul Stevens, *The Abolition of the Laity: Vocation, Work and Ministry in a Biblical Perspective*, Paternoster, 1999, chapter 7, in which Stevens takes up this idea and outlines three dimensions of the priestly ministry for the people of God.

7   Jim Thornton and Jorj Kowszun, *Witness at Work*, Church Home Group Resources Ltd, 1998, p62.

8   For further information on Lighthouses of Prayer, see their web site at *www.lighthousereport.com* (accessed October 2001).

9   See Nahum for a good example of prophecy about a city, in this case Nineveh. See Amos chapters 1 and 2 for prophecies concerning other nations, in this case Israel's neighbours. See Daniel for some prophecies to individuals, in this case the kings Nebuchadnezzar and Belshazzar.

10   The shift from corporate to individual prophecy in the church is often linked to the rise of the Kansas City Prophets in the early 1990s.

11   Drane, *McDonaldization*, p171.

12   Stevens, *Abolition*, p171.

13   Forster, the Baptist's Mainstream Conference, Swanwick 2001.

14   Grenz, *Primer*, p167.

15   Grenz, *Primer*, p172.

16   Thomas is often referred to as 'doubting Thomas' because of his reluctance to believe in the resurrection of Jesus (John 20:24–28)

Other Resources from Scripture Union

Christian Life and Today's World package
(Video editor: Rob Purbrick)
ISBN 1 85999 576 4

How can we take up the challenge of living as Christians in a postmodern society? From SU and LBC comes another stimulating small group resource containing video, accompanying workbook for group leaders and book of articles written by members of the LBC faculty.

A format pb 192pp + workbook 60pp + video £25.00

Light from a Dark Star
Where's God when my world falls apart?
Wayne Kirkland
ISBN: 1 85999 515 2, £4.99

It's the big question that won't go away. Why does God allow suffering? There are no simple answers in this book. No attempts to shrug off the serious challenges to faith which the question raises. Rather it engages compassionately with the sufferings of real people, grappling with slippery issues, in a discovery of some intriguing perspectives.

Knowing God's Ways
A user's guide to the Old Testament
Patton Taylor
ISBN: 1 85999 349 4, £6.99

Do you find the Old Testament difficult to get into? If you've been looking for some help in making sense of it all, then this book by a professor at Union Theological College in Belfast is what you've been looking for! His accessible, user-friendly approach will help you gain a clear overview of the Old Testament, understand different genres, and apply biblical teaching to today's world.

Journey into the Bible
John Drane
ISBN: 1 85999 409 1, £4.99

In his usual thought-provoking and accessible style John Drane gives a stimulating introduction to many of the issues raised by reading the Bible today. Designed especially for those who are struggling to come to terms with the Bible.

Dangerous Praying
Inspirational Ideas for individuals and groups
David Spriggs
ISBN: 1 85999335 4, £6.99

Drawing on Paul's letter to the Ephesians, this creative book challenges us to be bold when we pray, both in what we pray for and how we pray. David Spriggs presents us with 101 practical ideas and strategies to help us develop a courageous prayer life, whether in a group or individually.

Ready to Grow
Practical steps to knowing God better
Alan Harkness

ISBN 0 949720 71 2, £5.99

An attractive and practical book to encourage believers to make time with God a regular part of their lives. Includes chapters on preparation, getting started, the practicalities, sharing what you have learned, and different methods of combining Bible reading and prayer.

Faith and Common Sense
Living boldly, choosing wisely
David Dewey

ISBN: 1 85999 302 8, £4.99

This unusual book explores how we can live riskily yet sensibly. Drawing on the lives of key Bible characters like Peter, the author first lays a solid biblical and theological foundation for achieving a balance. Then follows a practical look at areas in our lives where a need for that balance is vital - healing, the gifts of the Spirit, work, money, failure and guidance.

The Bible Unwrapped
Developing your Bible skills
David Dewey

ISBN: 1 85999 533 0, £5.99

Is the Bible something of a closed book to you? Here you'll find help in finding your way around the Bible, and in grasping the big picture of the Bible's message. You'll also learn to appreciate the different types of literature in the Bible and be introduced to eight different approaches to Bible study. Clear and accurate charts and diagrams and a helpful glossary add value.

Understanding the Bible

John Stott
A format pb 192pp £2.99
ISBN 1 85999 225 0

A special budget edition of a widely-acclaimed classic bestseller. Outstanding Christian teacher and author John Stott examines the cultural, social, geographical and historical background of the Bible, outlining the story and explaining the message.

Understanding the Bible

John Stott
245x160mm hb 170pp £9.99
1 85999 569 1

A brand new edition in full colour. Revised and updated text is illustrated with charts, diagrams and wonderful colour photos. An ideal gift!

Bodybuilders
Small group resource

A highly relational small group resource that's flexible and fun to use. Six outlines in each book contain notes for leaders, prayer and worship ideas, photocopiable sheets of interactive and in-depth Bible study material and ideas for personal study during the week.

A Fresh Encounter (David Bolster) 1 85999 586 1

Designed for Great Things
(Anton Bauhmohl) 1 85999 585 3

Living for the King ('Tricia Williams) 1 85999 584 5

Relationship Building (Lance Pierson) 1 85999 582 9

Surviving Under Pressure (Christopher Griffiths & Stephen Hathway) 1 85999 587 X

Growing Through Change (Lance Pierson) 1 85999 583 7

210x140mm pb 32pp   £3.50

Equipped for living

New 2002

Florence MacKenzie

A series of four books designed for Christians wanting in-depth Bible study in an engaging, personal style. Thought-provoking questions for personal reflection and application to life as well as for group discussion. Between eight and ten studies in each book, illustrated by quotes from a wide variety of authors.

Living out the life of Jesus: The Fruit of the Spirit
1 85999 430 X

Living the kingdom lifestyle: The Beatitudes
1 85999 460 1

Living empowered for ministry: The Gifts of the Spirit
1 85999 458 X

Living under God's protection: The Armour of God
1 85999 450 4

All 210mmx140mm 80pp £3.50

Think outside the box...

Studying at London Bible College means...

- thinking deeply and laterally about your faith...

- growing in understanding of God and his word...

- developing your gifts and integrating academic study and practical skills...

- challenging your presuppositions, your prejudices and your traditions...

...live inside the kingdom.

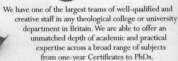

We have one of the largest teams of well-qualified and creative staff in any theological college or university department in Britain. We are able to offer an unmatched depth of academic and practical expertise across a broad range of subjects from one-year Certificates to PhDs.

And all of this within the enriching experience of living and studying in an international, multi-denominational, evangelical community.

Learn to live inside the kingdom.
Think outside the box. Think LBC.

For a prospectus or more information on our courses, contact Wendy Bales at London Bible College, Green Lane, Northwood, HA6 2UW. Tel: 01923 456 000 · Fax: 01923 456 001
E-mail: candr02@londonbiblecollege.ac.uk · Web: www.londonbiblecollege.ac.uk

CertHE · DipHE · BTh · BA · MA · MTh · MPhil · PhD · Open Learning · Counselling · Music & Worship

Theology@LBC

CENTRE FOR UNDERGRADUATE AND POSTGRADUATE THEOLOGICAL STUDIES

REGISTERED CHARITY NO. 312778 · LBC IS AN ASSOCIATED COLLEGE OF BRUNEL UNIVERSITY